Living with Moral Disagreement

Living with Moral Disagreement

The Enduring Controversy about Affirmative Action

MICHELE S. MOSES

The University of Chicago Press
Chicago and London

Michele S. Moses is professor of educational foundations, policy, and practice and associate dean for graduate studies in the School of Education at the University of Colorado Boulder. She is the author of *Embracing Race* and coeditor of *Affirmative Action Matters*.

The University of Chicago Press, Chicago 60637
The University of Chicago Press, Ltd., London
© 2016 by The University of Chicago
All rights reserved. Published 2016.
Printed in the United States of America

25 24 23 22 21 20 19 18 17 16   1 2 3 4 5

ISBN-13: 978-0-226-34424-9 (cloth)
ISBN-13: 978-0-226-34438-6 (paper)
ISBN-13: 978-0-226-34441-6 (e-book)
DOI: 10.7208/chicago/9780226344416.001.0001

Library of Congress Cataloging-in-Publication Data

Moses, Michele S., author.
    Living with moral disagreement : the enduring controversy about affirmative action / Michele S. Moses.
        pages ; cm
    Includes bibliographical references and index.
    ISBN 978-0-226-34424-9 (cloth : alk. paper) — ISBN 978-0-226-34438-6 (pbk. : alk. paper) — ISBN 978-0-226-34441-6 (e-book) 1. Affirmative action programs in education—United States. 2. Affirmative action programs in education—Government policy—United States. 3. Educational equalization—United States. 4. Education and state—United States. 5. Discrimination in education—United States. I. Title.
    LC213.52.M67 2016
    379.2'60973—dc23
                                                                    2015022450

♾ This paper meets the requirements of ANSI/NISO Z39.48-1992 (Permanence of Paper).

This book is dedicated to Chris, my love.

CONTENTS

ACKNOWLEDGMENTS

My father died suddenly while I was writing this book. In so many ways it was he who inspired my love of philosophy—not explicitly, perhaps, but in spirit—with his persistent questioning of my ideas and arguments, often challenging, sometimes flat-out disagreeing, but always open to learning something from his little girl. I miss him every day.

Disagreement. It can certainly be negative, but what comes along with it in the best of circumstances—dialogue, discussion, deliberation, greater understanding—are crucial parts of democracy. It is these things I hope we can foster when moral disagreements about education policy surface, particularly about race-conscious policies like affirmative action, which is the central policy discussed in this book.

While of course the ideas, mistakes, and arguments herein are mine alone, I would like to acknowledge the support I have received along the way: intellectual, financial, professional, and personal. In the first stages of this work, I was fortunate to have a National Academy of Education/Spencer Foundation Postdoctoral Fellowship, as well as a small grant from the National Forum on Higher Education for the Public Good. Later research grants from the Spencer Foundation and the University of Colorado Boulder LEAP, Grant-in-Aid, Center to Advance Research and Teaching in the Social Sciences Scholars Fund, and IMPART grants programs made the development of this book manuscript possible. I want to thank my dean at the University of Colorado Boulder School of Education, Lorrie Shepard, who was always flexible when I needed writing time, even when as one of her associate deans, she needed my assistance on administrative or student matters. She has been in my corner since I was a new doctoral student in her Doctoral Seminar course. I am proud to say that she is a dean who supports humanities-oriented scholarship in an education research culture increasingly prone to ignoring such work. In the later stages of this work, Elizabeth Branch Dyson encouraged me to refine the ideas for consideration by the University of Chicago Press, and I am so lucky to have worked on this project with her and all the editors and assistants at Chicago. I am very grateful for all of this support.

I want to acknowledge that parts of chapters 2, 3, 4, and 5 appeared originally in several academic journals: they are substantially revised for inclusion here. Parts of an article with John Yun and Patricia Marin, "Affirmative Action's Fate: Are 20 More Years Enough?" in *Education Policy Analysis Archives* 17 (17) (2009), were revised and expanded for inclusion in chapter 2. Chapter 3 combines revisions of relevant pieces from the following articles: "Why the Affirmative Action Debate Persists: The Role of Moral Disagreement," in *Educational Policy* 20 (4) (2006): 567–86; "Contested Ideals: Understanding Moral Disagreements over Education Policy," in *Journal of Social Philosophy* 35 (4) (2004): 471–82; and "Moral and Instrumental Rationales for Affirmative Action in Five National Contexts," in *Educational Researcher* 39 (3) (2010): 211–28. Chapter 4 began as a paper I gave at the Philosophy of Education Society Annual Meeting: "By the People, for the People: Interrogating the Education-Policy-by-Ballot-Initiative Phenomenon," which was published in *Philosophy of Education 2009*, edited by Deborah Kerdeman, 177–86 (Urbana, IL: Philosophy of Education Society, 2010). Pieces of this chapter also appeared originally in an article with Lauren P. Saenz, "When the Majority Rules: Ballot Initiatives, Race-Conscious Education Policy, and the Public Good," which was published in *Review of Research in Education* 36 (1) (2012): 113–38, edited by Kathryn Borman, Arnold Danzig, and David R. Garcia. Finally, chapter 5 is a quite different version of an article written with Lauren P. Saenz and Amy N. Farley: "The Central Role of Philosophy in a Study of Community Dialogues," in *Studies in Philosophy and Education* 34 (2) (2015): 193–203.

As I have been working on these ideas for some time, parts of the manuscript draw on previous research projects. In particular I draw on research from my Deliberative Dialogues research project, conducted in collaboration with Ken Howe, Lauren Saenz, Amy Farley Lobue, Kristen Davidson, Jarrod Hanson, Darrell Jackson, Mike Seymour, and Adam Van Iwaarden, wonderful colleagues, educators, and researchers. I have very much appreciated discussions, feedback, and insightful comments on various chapter drafts from Chris Bell, Gabriela Bell, Nicolas Bell, Amy Farley Lobue, Peter French, Jarrod Hanson, Cathy Horn, Bethy Leonardi, Patricia Marin, David Meens, Christina Paguyo, Lauren Saenz, Katy Wiley, and John Yun. And, of course, from Ken Howe, who has always, always been there for me as a mentor, friend, and colleague, from the moment I walked into his office more than twenty years ago and asked him whether he needed help with a book on equal educational opportunity he was working on at the time. I am so glad I knocked on his door. (He didn't need my help, by the way, but I certainly needed his.)

Finally, the past ten years of friendship with Elizabeth Dutro have made all the difference in my professional and personal life, and I owe her much gratitude for every bit of encouragement along the way. My parents, Maria and John Moses, have helped me in ways impossible to quantify, and I can never ever thank them enough. My children, Gabriela and Nicolas, were always understanding about my balance between work and family, and they are both amazing philosophers and critics, always wanting to learn, ask questions, and have fun with new ideas. Most of all, because of them work has not taken over; there has been wonderful time for travel, cooking, reading, volleyball, games, tennis, music, theatre, camping, and just being together as a family. And Chris, who listened to me go on and on about how to make sense of the puzzles of moral disagreement, who sat with me at a little restaurant in Phoenix when the central question finally began to take shape, who celebrated every chapter drafted, and who is always fun and interesting to talk and hang out with—thank you.

ONE

"Who *Isn't* for Equality?"

As I have written before,[1] I am an unapologetic supporter of affirmative action. I am also a defender of related race-conscious education policies, which I view as both morally just and justifiable. But I understand why other educational and political theorists and philosophers might not agree with me. I do not think affirmative action is a perfect policy. I wish we in the United States did not need it. This makes me puzzled about how to understand the nature of the deep disagreement about affirmative action and, beyond that, what to do about it. Because although I can understand the nature and consequences of the disagreement, I still think that affirmative action is a right-headed policy for the society in which we currently live. I still think that it fosters meaningful opportunities for students of color.[2] I still think that we need it as one policy tool that moves us toward a more just and democratic society.

At first, the idea for this book was to add to the literature on race-conscious education policies, providing a philosophical perspective that supporters could use in their own work. In the course of working on these ideas, however, my state was targeted by an anti-affirmative action ballot initiative. Wanting to lend my expertise on the subject to public discussions about the policy and the ballot initiative, I worked with a team of scholars at my institution to develop opportunities for small community dialogue sessions on the issue of affirmative action. At the same time, we studied the dialogues themselves and how the participants seemed to take them up. The results of that research (the focus of chapter 5) complicated my views on how and why to discuss affirmative action policy. I became less focused on sharing yet another defense of the policy, less focused on completely changing the minds of the policy's opponents. I came to see the deep democratic value of policy dialogue and deliberation. Regardless of whether participants decided to support or oppose affirmative action after the dialogue session, they were more *informed*, and more *civil* to those with whom they disagreed, after the experience. Some deliberative forums seek to bring the participants to consensus, which certainly can be an appropriate aim. In some cases of deep moral disagreement, however, I think it is important to understand dialogue and deliberation as *expanding* people's minds and hearts rather than necessarily *changing* them wholesale. Information and deeper thinking about controversial issues help people better understand the issues as well as each other's views, and in cases where a policy vote or decision is involved, people may be better able to vote as they intend and not be tricked by the campaign messages or propaganda (Moses et al. 2010). For example, one of the participants in our community dialogues on affirmative action explored with the group how difficult it can be to tease out the meaning of policy proposals that invoke democratic ideals: "after all who *isn't* for equality, and it [anti-affirmative action ballot initiative Amendment 46] is written so that most people just get a brush past the thing and assume that it's not about affirmative action, it just stands for equality and I'm all for it." Both critics and defenders of affirmative action in Colorado were using the ideal of equality to make their (opposing) arguments about affirmative action policy. This participant put his finger on a central issue in the acrimonious debates over race-conscious affirmative action: how can citizens make sense of the policy within a sociopolitical context where both supporters and opponents use the same language to defend or critique it?

Given all that, this book is not meant to be another defense of affirmative action. It *will* be a defense of dialogue and deliberation about affirmative action and other controversial race-conscious policies. Disagreements such as these are inevitable in a democracy; the key to a thriving democracy—or so I argue—is citizens' ability to discuss these disagreements, to work to understand the values and beliefs that undergird the differences. I focus on the importance of dialogue for allowing us to stand in others' shoes and for seeing each other's humanity despite disagreement. Such dialogue is the heart of both education and democracy. Maybe dialogue and deliberation will not always (or even often) lead to agreement in policy issues related to moral views, but they have the potential to help us know each other and to understand each other better amidst disagreement. We learn through dialogue that we do not have all the answers, and this mitigates agonism. In that vein, one participant discussed what she learned about affirmative action from the dialogue: "I wasn't really sure that I had an opinion either way on it just because I wasn't terribly informed and I think going to the forum helped me understand that there are ramifications to a lot of these kinds of amendments and ballot initiatives that aren't necessarily obvious on the face of the initiative itself and that kind of educating yourself and getting different viewpoints is helpful in making sure you are making an informed vote." As this participant implied, people are able to get beyond their sometimes-narrow perspectives to understand the complexity of the different views on affirmative action policy. If this leads us to understanding that we have more to learn, that is a good outcome for a more civil democratic society. I believe that dialogues centering on the moral disagreements about public policy will contribute to greater civic respect and appreciation for diverse values and stances; however, I also believe that such dialogues can lead to shifts in opinions about race-conscious policies like affirmative action. These two outcomes are not mutually exclusive, as both are possible outcomes of a greater understanding of moral disagreement and of democratic dialogues. We cannot be sure what the outcomes of dialogue about policy disagreements will be, but it is possible (and empirical research has shown) that sometimes dialogues lead to greater civic respect and understanding of others' points of view, sometimes participants will even shift their views, and sometimes both will occur.

To be clear, I still think there is a right answer about affirmative action—ethically; indeed the preponderance of evidence points toward affirmative action fostering educational opportunities worth wanting[3] (Anderson 2010; Howe 1997; Jacobs 2004; Moses 2002) as well as more racially and ethnically diverse social and educational institutions (Chang 2001; Garces 2013b; Kidder 2012, 2013; Moses, Yun, and Marin 2009; Vega 2014). But I also understand that not everyone will agree with my conclusion. My scholarly position on affirmative action is certainly relevant to understanding my arguments in this book; I am not claiming to study moral disagreement about race-conscious education policies without taking a side on the affirmative action debate. One might point out that my scholarly position might undermine my broader argument for the importance of dialogue about policy. Yet, as I mention earlier, my arguments here were inspired partially by my experiences with community dialogues on affirmative action.[4] Through such dialogues, like the participants I was willing to listen to arguments opposing affirmative action. Although they have not caused me to change my stance wholesale, I have learned to be much more understanding and respectful of such views. And ultimately I have come to see that the moral disagreement about affirmative action has brought about some reasonable compromises about the policy that have strengthened its capacity to function as one tool that colleges and universities can use to build more equitable educational opportunities.

I also try to make the case that such disagreements are crucial for democratic politics. I do not think that my own position undermines my overall point; in fact, I am an example of a citizen who has benefited from dialogue about the policy. I still support affirmative action, but I now believe that the disagreement about it has led to reasonable policy compromises in some cases, albeit not in the states where affirmative action ballot initiatives bans have passed. Those are not actually compromises, but more of what I discuss in chapter 4 as the imposition of one person's or a few powerful, wealthy people's views. Ultimately, policies still have to be made and we still have to live together in this democratic society. So we have to talk with each other and learn about each other enough so that we can, if not agree, at least understand each other's views on debatable topics even as we continue to argue for what is morally right. One big question I tackle in this book is how educators and other stakeholders should deal with disagreements about education policy issues that appear to be intractable, that is, resistant to easy solutions or compromises.

The book comes at a moment in US history defined by the first black president, as well as by discussions of whether race still matters in public life, and a shift in the debates over how best to address issues of equality of educational opportunity—equity-focused policies or achievement-focused policies. Within this sociopolitical context, the disagreement about affirmative action in higher education admissions continues, most significantly through state ballot initiatives and court challenges. To improve the deliberation over affirmative action and retain hope for a mutually acceptable resolution of the moral controversy, I make the case that stakeholders in the policy process must understand the moral and political underpinnings of the debate over policies like affirmative action. As US Supreme Court Justice Sandra Day O'Connor suggested in the *Grutter v. Bollinger* majority opinion, increasing access to higher education through affirmative action is justified by a commitment to a diverse democracy (*Grutter* 2003, 330–32). I agree, and I hope this book sheds some light on what I take to be the persistent *moral* disagreement about affirmative action's role in our democratic society, so that concepts such as equality of educational opportunity can be understood in a meaningful way, rather than merely as slogans that can be endorsed easily by people with quite different ideological perspectives and policy ideas.

Aims of the Book

My primary purposes for writing this book are twofold. First, I aim to provide a philosophical analysis of the enduring moral disagreement about affirmative action in light of court rulings and pieces of state legislation related to affirmative action and race-conscious education policy. I seek to make sense of the different policy prescriptions that emerge despite prima facie agreement on foundational political ideals. Although I do not try to conceal my own position in support of affirmative action, I also do not rehearse the pros and cons about this policy once more. Instead, I hope my examination will increase understanding about the values and beliefs that underlie the complex pro and con positions through the analysis of affirmative action as an example of a moral disagreement. Second, I aim to contribute to the scholarly conversation about the role of disagreement in democracy and how education scholars can participate in and promote public dialogue and deliberation around issues of deep moral disagreement. Affirmative action provides an analytically interesting instance of controversial race-conscious education policy that has profound implications for equality and diversity in higher education. Thus, I bring political philosophy to bear on reshaping the scholarly conversation around affirmative action, with implications for other deeply contested education policy issues that affect equality of educational opportunity.

Regarding my methods, philosophical inquiry contributes to scholarship in education by clarifying arguments and analyzing just how policies like affirmative action and concepts like equality are related. Although such questions and their analyses do not submit themselves easily to measurement, they challenge empirical researchers to think in new and careful ways about what the important questions are around race-conscious policies and how and what can be effectively measured and analyzed. In this way, philosophy and theory building serve as important companions to empirical analyses and rationales for race consciousness in education, by examining less tangible factors like moral values and ideals that are part of the foundation of policy debates. Daniel Vokey (2009) describes such conceptual work in philosophy of education as "critically comparing the competing sets of fundamental philosophical and other beliefs ('worldviews') that accompany radically different conceptions of the proper ends and means of education" (339). To ground the more abstract analyses, I also apply political theory in an examination of relevant empirical data from a study I conducted of community dialogues on affirmative action policy. The intent of the study was to learn how such an educative and deliberative effort affected participants' information and beliefs about affirmative action. This examination flows into my concluding arguments about the role of moral disagreement in US society, for the importance of public deliberation and education in controversial matters of education policy, and for the role of education scholars in providing evidence-based information to the public.

As such, this work is an instance of non-ideal theory, that is, philosophical work that carefully considers and takes into account the decidedly non-ideal sociopolitical contexts and circumstances present in the real world, characterized by unequal and unjust social structures. Yet I hope that it is also an instance of what philosopher of education Ken Howe calls *ambitious* non-ideal theory, that is, grounded in reality, but also trying to envision the world beyond the status quo, and how we might go about getting to more equitable and just education policies.[5] As battles against affirmative action and related policies continue not only in the courts but also in the court of public opinion, philosophical issues become more central to public discussion and deliberation.

Specific programs may differ from one another, but affirmative action policy most often aims to diversify institutions of higher education by taking an applicant's race, ethnicity, and gender into account in making selection decisions. In the United States, this means that if an applicant is African American, Latino/a, Asian American, Native American, and/or female, this fact is taken as one qualifying factor among many considered in admissions or hiring processes. The range of affirmative action programs is broad, from federal contracts to employment and promotion, to college and university admissions. Resting on the affirmative action policies in Executive Order 11246 and Title VI of the Civil Rights Act of 1964, which specify that discrimination by race, color, religion, sex, or national origin is prohibited by agencies receiving federal funding, many businesses, public agencies, and institutions of higher education began to revise their admissions and hiring policies so that a broader pool of people could have increased educational and employment opportunities.

Arguments for and against affirmative action have certainly been made, including my own.[6] My intent here is to go beyond those arguments to get at the deeper moral and political conflicts that shape how we view what justice requires of education policy. What is needed—and what I attempt to tackle—is an examination of the moral and political underpinnings of the disagreement. Little, if any, philosophy of education scholarship is undertaking this difficult problem. A deeper understanding of the nature of the disagreement over race-conscious education policies constitutes an important step toward negotiating policies that honor educational opportunities for all students. Progress is unlikely if the disputants continue to talk past one another.

Because the US Supreme Court ruled in 2003 in *Grutter v. Bollinger* that it is constitutional for colleges and universities to consider race and ethnicity in admissions decisions, and the court did not take the opportunity to strike down the *Grutter* precedent ten years later in *Fisher v. University of Texas* (remanding the case back to the lower court), it might seem that examinations of affirmative action and related race-conscious policies no longer would be necessary. The highest court in the land decided that diversity is a compelling state interest and that narrowly tailored affirmative action plans are acceptable ways for colleges and universities to foster that diversity. However, the disagreement about affirmative action has never been related to straightforward questions of what the law allows. If that were the case, then the 1978 *Regents of the University of California v. Bakke* decision affirming the constitutionality of the consideration of race in college and university admissions decisions ought to have put out the fires of controversy. I have come to see the debates over affirmative action and other race-conscious education policies as moral disagreements that stem not only from factors such as racism but also—and importantly—from differing conceptions of central democratic ideals, in particular equality, liberty, and diversity. These in turn are the result of profound theoretical disagreements between those who believe that democratic ideals require equal opportunity policies like affirmative action and those who believe that similar or parallel ideals require abolishing them. This examination allows us to think more carefully about why we in the United States cannot agree about race-conscious policies like affirmative action and helps us go beyond knee-jerk responses (e.g., "if you don't support it, you're racist"; "if you do support it, you're a bleeding heart") to better understand the multiple facets of the debate, as well as how we might reach mutual understanding regarding the larger moral disagreement surrounding such policies.

Chapter Overview

In the chapters to follow, I first describe the case of affirmative action in higher education as setting the stage for moral disagreement. I use examples of key court cases and legislation for two purposes: first, to inform readers of the complex policy landscape in which my arguments land, and second, to show how all of the back and forth between judges or policymakers in the decades-long debates about affirmative action mirrors the public disagreement exemplified by the different interpretations of the ideals discussed in chapter 3. As such, this chapter begins with an overview of the larger legal, political, and legislative context of the affirmative action case. It demonstrates how the moral disagreement about affirmative action plays out in political practice as those on both sides of the debate fight to have their vision of equality instantiated by policy. The landscape is complicated by the use of both legal avenues and legislative avenues, and chapter 2 examines each of these.

Next I focus on the nature of moral disagreement in general and about affirmative action in particular. Chapter 3 examines how the ideals of equality and liberty may conflict, as well as the related ideal of diversity, in an effort to understand the moral and political roots of education policy disagreements. I make the case that understanding the nature of moral disagreement enriches the discussion of specific policy controversies that have implications for equity and social justice. To clarify the terms of moral disagreement, I use affirmative action as a case study to examine how the broad political theories of justice that dominate the debate—egalitarian political theory and libertarian political theory—interpret the moral ideals of equality and liberty. I also examine the most prominent rationales for affirmative action policy as examples of how the dominant political theories play out in justifying affirmative action.

In chapter 4, I take a closer look at the most commonly used legislative avenue for influencing affirmative action policy: the use of state ballot initiatives to eliminate affirmative action. I view the state ballot initiative as an example of direct democracy used to further libertarian opposition to race-conscious education policies. Ballot initiatives themselves illustrate the differences between egalitarian and libertarian political theory. And the campaigns for and against the anti-affirmative action instances of such ballot initiatives provide important instances of how those differences play out within the practical political arena.

Next I move to an investigation of how philosophers of education and education researchers might make inroads into understanding and mitigating the moral disagreement over race-conscious education policies through democratic deliberation, with an examination of a series of community dialogues my research team and I facilitated on the topic of affirmative action in the context of an anti-affirmative action state ballot initiative. As such, in chapter 5 I apply the moral and political theories to the analysis of these data and examine the relationships among moral disagreement, education policy, and public dialogue. I also present analyses of questionnaires and follow-up interviews with dialogue participants. These dialogues provide a promising method for members of the community to better understand each other's moral and political values and positions, without necessarily coming to consensus.

Finally, in the context of the theoretical and empirical work presented in the previous chapters, chapter 6 concludes the book with a discussion of whether it is possible to transcend the profound moral disagreements over education policy. I discuss the importance of disagreement and deliberation for fostering mutual respect as well as democracy. I hope the ideas and topics herein speak to other scholars—that is "experts"—who can use their expertise to inform the public about important education policy matters. Ultimately, I argue for an active role for scholars in fostering public deliberation and greater understanding of others' values and perspectives. More dialogue and better understanding will foster more equitable and democratic policies. It may not be *the* antidote to the polarized, dismissive, combative, and argumentative stances often assumed by scholars and stakeholders in the midst of moral disagreement, but without it the promise of democratic education and politics will remain unfulfilled.

TWO

The Case of Affirmative Action Policy

In this chapter, I delve more deeply into the specifics of the affirmative action case. The legal, political, and legislative contexts of this policy illustrate the moral and political nature of the disagreement about affirmative action and other controversial race-conscious education policies. What is particularly interesting about the case of affirmative action as a moral disagreement, and the numerous court cases and legislative actions that have accompanied it, is all of the flipping back and forth on the issue. Disagreements among the US Supreme Court justices highlight the different interpretations of the ideals of equality, liberty, and diversity that I examine in chapter 3, and, as such, they parallel the public disagreement as well.

Policy Background

In the last several years, various events and incidents have sparked reexamination of the role of race in American life. Some of these turns were promising, and others were painful reminders of how far we have to go. And they all seemed to take place simultaneously. For example, the governor of Virginia, Bob McDonnell, has declared April to be Confederate History Month in his state. When civil rights leaders criticized the move, Governor McDonnell explained that his proclamation was designed to promote tourism (Kumar and Helderman 2010). The 2008 election brought not only the first black president of the United States but also the first viable female candidate. In another first, in 2009, a Latina was nominated and confirmed as a justice on the Supreme Court. During Sonia Sotomayor's confirmation hearing, Senator Tom Coburn of Oklahoma told the nominee that she would "have lots of 'splainin' to do" for her views, invoking Ricky Ricardo from the television series *I Love Lucy* (Rich 2009, ¶ 4, line 5). Also in 2009, Professor

Henry Louis Gates was arrested while trying to enter his own home, triggering a new round of race analyses in so-called postracial America. "'I can't wear my Harvard gown everywhere I go.' Professor Gates said. 'We—all of us in the crossover generation—have multiple identities, and being black trumps all of those other identities'" (Cooper 2009, ¶ 21, lines 1–3). During President Barack Obama's first campaign for the presidency, another campaign was also launched by Ward Connerly and his group, the American Civil Rights Institute, for what Connerly called "Super Tuesday for Equal Rights," to promote five state ballot initiatives that, if passed, would eliminate affirmative action in Arizona, Colorado, Missouri, Nebraska, and Oklahoma. The initiatives made it onto the ballots in Colorado and Nebraska; ultimately, Nebraska followed California, Michigan, and Washington to become the fourth state to abolish affirmative action in public education, employment, and contracting. The same initiative passed in Arizona in 2010 and Oklahoma in 2012, the same year President Obama was reelected. Most recently, the Project on Fair Representation is suing both the University of North Carolina at Chapel Hill and Harvard University on behalf of students who claim they were discriminated against based on race in the admissions process (CBS 2014). The student plaintiffs were recruited actively by affirmative action opponent Edward Blum, who was also behind the *Fisher v. University of Texas* case that I discuss below (McCloskey 2014).[1]

The debate over affirmative action, particularly in higher education admissions, has been a consistent part of the larger analysis of race in the United States. Notably, in 2013, the US Supreme Court made a somewhat unexpected ruling in the *Fisher v. University of Texas* case concerning the use of affirmative action in admissions at the state's flagship campus of the University of Texas at Austin. White plaintiffs who had been rejected for undergraduate admissions sued the university. They lost in US district court, but appealed the decision to the US Supreme Court. In response, the Obama administration filed an amicus brief taking a strong stance in favor of affirmative action in higher education admissions citing the educational and social benefits of a racially and ethnically diverse student body (Jaschik 2010b). Although the brief itself did not invoke egalitarianism specifically, such a position stems from a race-egalitarian philosophy, with the understanding that race and ethnicity continue to play a significant role in American society. Part of the importance of affirmative action is that it is used primarily in the most selective institutions of higher education, the very places that educate many of our nation's leaders, officeholders, and professionals. The state of the US public education system is such that many students of color are underserved and consequently not as competitive in their college applications (Yosso et al. 2004). For example, black and Latino students are underrepresented in Advanced Placement programs (Jaschik 2010a) and in college preparatory courses in general. Such realities lead to the underrepresentation of students of color in selective colleges and universities. This, in turn, produces a dearth of scientists of color, lawyers of color, and doctors of color, to name a few examples (Haycock, Lynch, and Engle 2009; *JBHE* 2010). Research has shown that without affirmative action, selective colleges and universities would suffer significant decreases in enrollment of underrepresented students of color (Hinrichs 2009, 2012; Howell 2010; Long 2007; Long and Tienda 2008). The most selective and prestigious University of California campuses did, in fact, suffer this drop-off after affirmative action policies were banned in that state, even though the number of underrepresented minority students graduating from high school increased (Moses, Yun, and Marin 2009; Saenz 2010). Similarly, undergraduate enrollment of black students at the University of Michigan decreased to 4.6 percent in 2013 (Vega 2014)—this in a state with a 14.3 percent black population (United States Census Bureau 2013). Still, these realities fail to stem the deep disagreement about affirmative action, which, as I examine in chapter 3, is characterized by the conflicting paradigms of race egalitarianism and color blindness.

Instead of taking the opportunity in *Fisher* to strike down the constitutionality of using race in higher education admissions decisions, the court remanded the case to the lower court to rule on the question of whether the university's admissions program that considers race is narrowly tailored to obtain the benefits of a diverse student body.

The Case of Affirmative Action

In the United States, affirmative action in higher education admissions primarily relates to race, ethnicity, and gender. Quotas are rarely if ever used, based on the *Regents of the University of California v. Bakke* ruling against quotas and set-aside places at universities. *Gratz v. Bollinger* reinforced the impermissibility for numeric set-asides in university admissions, and *Grutter v. Bollinger* upheld the constitutionality of affirmative action (Moses, Yun, and Marin 2009). This conceptualization of affirmative action without quotas evolved over its fifty-year history in the United States (Moses 2002).

Because the Supreme Court has allowed universities to use affirmative action policies, opponents have turned to another strategy to ban such policies, the state-level ballot initiative (Moses and Saenz 2008). Such initiatives to abolish affirmative action in the targeted state have been proposed in nine states, placed on the ballot in seven, passed in six (Arizona, California,

Michigan, Nebraska, Oklahoma, and Washington), and defeated in one (Colorado) (Farley, Gaertner, and Moses 2013; Marin 2014). In what follows, I first discuss the key court cases shaping the landscape of affirmative action policy. Then I examine the state ballot initiatives and other state legislation that have eliminated or have intended to eliminate affirmative action in those states. Along with chapter 3, this will provide the legal and political context to inform chapter 4's analysis of how the turn toward direct democratic ballot initiatives—as well as the campaigns for and against them—relies on ideas and ideals from egalitarian and libertarian political theory.

The controversy over affirmative action has resulted in numerous important court cases and legislative actions that not only have shaped the contours of the policy but also exemplify the public moral disagreement about it. Although I will not examine each case in detail herein, I have chosen to explore key cases and legislation that demonstrate the different interpretations of the ideals of equality and liberty that shape the disagreement. Through a concurrent review of key court rulings and state legislation, I present analyses of some key federal court decisions regarding affirmative action in higher education admissions: *Regents of the University of California v. Bakke* (1978), *Hopwood v. Texas* (1996), *Gratz v. Bollinger* (2003), *Grutter v. Bollinger* (2003), and *Fisher v. University of Texas* (2013).[2] I also include a relevant K–12 case insofar as it pertains to higher education, *Parents Involved in Community Schools v. Seattle School District No. 1* (2007).[3] In addition, I examine several state political and legal events: California's Proposition 209 (1996), Michigan's Proposal 2 (2006), and the ballot initiative campaign in Colorado.

Key Court Cases: Conflicting Values

Affirmative action causes a "conflicted public mind" (Sandel 2005, 101) due to the simultaneous desire for racial equality and color-blind policies. As I mention in the last chapter, the public mind has become no less conflicted as affirmative action policy has been tested and contested in the courts and at the ballot. These conflicts emerge as the justices of the Supreme Court have deliberated about the constitutionality of using race as a factor in college admissions decisions. I begin with the first case in which US Supreme Court justices ruled on affirmative action in higher education admissions.

Regents of the University of California v. Bakke

Prior to the 1978 US Supreme Court case *Regents of the University of California v. Bakke*, the national mood had been moving in favor of policies and programs designed to support equality of educational opportunity (Moses 2002). Great Society and War on Poverty programs were indicative of this mood. Yet the landmark *Bakke* case marks the beginning of a strong back-lash against race-conscious policies. Perhaps the case's most lasting policy effect was to clarify that the use of numeric quotas and set-aside places within admission programs seeking to promote diversity in higher educa-tion is forbidden because it violates the Fourteenth Amendment to the US Constitution. Even though the legal legacy of the *Bakke* case is significant, the decision itself was the result of a fractured Supreme Court. The justices held 4–1–4 that "(a) the minority-admissions program of the University of California at Davis Medical School had discriminated illegally against a white male applicant, but (b) that universities could legally consider race as a factor in admissions" (Sobel 1980, 145). Justices Warren Burger, John Paul Stevens, Potter Stewart, and William Rehnquist decided in favor of plaintiff Allan Bakke on both counts; Justices William Brennan, Byron White, Thur-good Marshall, and Harry Blackmun decided in favor of the University of California at Davis Medical School on both counts, and, in the swing vote, Justice Lewis Powell decided *against* the Davis policy, but *in favor of* univer-sities' ability to use race as a plus factor in admissions decisions. Although Powell was the only justice to use the educational benefits of diversity as his rationale in favor of race-conscious admissions policies, his became the court's controlling opinion since he cast the deciding vote for each side. Although its division illustrated the larger disagreement within US society, the Supreme Court indicated to the nation that affirmative action programs were constitutional and could be implemented legally. The four justices who were against both UC-Davis's quotas and the constitutionality of consider-ing race viewed affirmative action as degrading to the ideal of equality. The four justices in favor of affirmative action policy saw it as a legitimate way to further equality.

One especially enduring justification for affirmative action policies, the diversity rationale, came from Justice Powell's *Bakke* opinion. The legacy left by *Bakke* provided the legal guidelines for affirmative action policy, now updated and bolstered by *Grutter*, as discussed below. Although the diversity rationale for the use of affirmative action in higher education admissions remains in place within the legal framework, that fact has not precluded legal challenges to *Bakke*. The dispute over the nature of affirmative action and its consideration of race and ethnicity did not end with the *Bakke* ruling. The next important court case regarding higher education admissions was decided in 1996 with *Hopwood v. Texas*.

Hopwood v. Texas

In deciding *Hopwood*, the Court of Appeals for the Fifth Circuit ruled against race-conscious affirmative action policies in higher education admissions, thus nullifying the US Supreme Court's *Bakke* ruling in the three states in the Fifth Circuit: Texas, Louisiana, and Mississippi.[4] The white female plaintiff in the case, Cheryl Hopwood, relied on a strict interpretation of equality and equal (same) treatment, arguing that she had been discriminated against by the University of Texas Law School's admissions system. *Hopwood*'s three-judge panel agreed with this interpretation and ruled to prohibit the use of race-conscious admissions criteria to achieve diversity at the law school. The panel decided that a state's interest in acquiring a diverse student body was not legally compelling enough to justify an admissions program like the one at the law school. *Hopwood* was the first successful challenge to an affirmative action admissions program since *Bakke*. One year later, Texas Attorney General Dan Morales offered clarification on the *Hopwood* decision for the state, maintaining that its reach extended to programs outside of admissions, including financial aid, recruitment, and scholarships. Subsequent research on the impact of the decision concluded that *Hopwood* had a chilling effect on college access for black and Hispanic high school graduates in Texas (Dickson 2004; Kain and O'Brien 2001).

At the flagship University of Texas at Austin (UT-Austin), officials put a great deal of effort into implementing various policies and programs to mitigate the effect of losing affirmative action. In addition, the Texas legislature passed House Bill 508—the Top Ten Percent Plan—guaranteeing "admission to the top 10 percent of a high school graduating class to any public higher education institution in the state" (Marin and Flores 2008, 226).[5] However, once the US Supreme Court issued its 2003 rulings effectively overturning *Hopwood*, UT President Larry Faulkner indicated that the university would work with the Texas legislature to resume affirmative action policies (University of Texas at Austin 2003a). Having had the experience of operating without affirmative action, President Faulkner was eager to reinstitute the policy. Bruce Walker, vice provost and director of admissions at UT-Austin, said at the time, "We have used race-neutral policies for seven years and still do not have a critical mass of African American or Hispanic students in our classrooms" (University of Texas at Austin 2003b). Currently UT-Austin uses both race-conscious admissions policies as well as the Top Ten Percent Plan (Chapa and Horn 2007). The *Fisher* case, described later, is the most recent court challenge to UT-Austin's affirmative action policy.

Gratz v. Bollinger and Grutter v. Bollinger

The plaintiffs in *Gratz* and *Grutter* were white applicants who believed that they would have been admitted to the University of Michigan had it not been for the consideration of race/ethnicity in the institution's admissions decisions; Jennifer Gratz sued regarding the undergraduate admissions policy and Barbara Grutter regarding the law school admissions policy. Like Bakke's lawyers in 1978, the plaintiffs' Center for Individual Rights lawyers maintained that the University of Michigan's use of race as a factor in admissions violated the equal protection clause of the Fourteenth Amendment and Title VI of the Civil Rights Act. Again we see anti-affirmative action plaintiffs relying on the idea of equality as sameness, which comes out of a color-blind paradigm. In the final decision in these cases, issued June 23, 2003, the Supreme Court upheld Justice Powell's opinion in *Bakke* that student diversity is a compelling state interest. By upholding the University of Michigan Law School admissions policy as narrowly tailored, the court endorsed policies that follow its guidelines in letter and spirit. It upheld the constitutionality of using race and ethnicity as plus factors in higher education admissions decisions and emphasized the importance of individualized, holistic reviews of applications.

More specifically, in *Gratz*, the justices struck down the University of Michigan's particular race-conscious undergraduate admissions program, emphasizing that any type of quota or numerical point system that automatically awards points to minority applicants does not fall under the permissible standards regarding the use of race and ethnicity in admissions decisions. In its *Grutter* ruling the court affirmed that the educational benefits flowing from a diverse student body served a compelling state interest. The diversity rationale, based on the ideal of diversity in a democratic society, was the central justification in upholding the constitutionality of affirmative action. Writing for the majority in *Grutter*, Justice O'Connor explained: "The Law School's educational judgment that such diversity is essential to its educational mission is one to which we defer. The Law School's assessment that diversity will, in fact, yield educational benefits is substantiated by respondents and their *amici*" (*Grutter* 2003, 328). She also noted that policies could focus on a range of attributes including applicants' varied talents and experiences and possible contributions to the learning environment, as well as academic ability. The key would be to assess each applicant individually. In addition, the *Grutter* decision highlighted Justice O'Connor's idea that affirmative action should no longer be necessary in twenty-five years.[6]

Ultimately, the ruling in *Grutter* invalidated the Fifth Circuit's ruling in

Hopwood. The *Grutter* decision thus underscored the importance and legal viability of the diversity rationale for affirmative action in college and university admissions. This justification has wider appeal than the remedial justification, as even those who oppose affirmative action sometimes support the idea of diversity (see, e.g., Deardorff and Jones 2007[7]). In fact, even the plaintiffs in *Gratz v. Bollinger* did not contest the importance of diversity to higher education. In addition, the *Grutter* court emphasized that institutions should engage in holistic review of applicants, within which they consider both quantitative (e.g., high school grade point average) and qualitative (e.g., extracurricular activities) assessments of the applicant's qualifications for admission.

After these rulings, opponents of race-conscious education policies seemed to feel a renewed urgency to prohibit the consideration of race and ethnicity in higher education admissions and related programs. Immediately after the rulings in *Gratz* and *Grutter* were announced, Ward Connerly, chair of the American Civil Rights Coalition, announced that he would propose an amendment to Michigan's state constitution opposing affirmative action (see the section below about Proposal 2).

Parents Involved in Community Schools v. Seattle School District No. 1

Extending outside of higher education is a group of court cases involving K–12 race-conscious student assignment plans in public schools. Although these cases are important primarily for the K–12 arena, *Parents Involved in Community Schools v. Seattle School District No. 1* is probably the most relevant to higher education. In 2007 the US Supreme Court took up the issue of voluntary race-conscious student assignment in public schools when it agreed to hear *Parents Involved in Community Schools v. Seattle School District No. 1* and *Meredith v. Jefferson County Board of Education.*[8] The court had changed significantly in its composition since the 2003 University of Michigan cases. Chief Justice William Rehnquist had died and been replaced by similarly conservative Chief Justice John Roberts, whose views on race consciousness stem from libertarian political theory, with a focus on color blindness. In addition, Justice Sandra Day O'Connor had retired, and her spot was filled by Justice Samuel Alito. Justice O'Connor had moderate egalitarian leanings within a divided court and was often the swing vote in contentious cases such as *Grutter.* By contrast, Justice Alito was expected to align with his conservative colleagues on the high court. It was not surprising, then, when the Supreme Court ruled that voluntary racial integration plans in place in school districts in Seattle and Louisville were not narrowly tailored and, thus, unconstitutional (Korrell 2007). However, the decision left the *Grutter* ruling intact and supported the idea of diversity as a compelling interest in both higher education and K–12.

Fisher v. University of Texas at Austin

In another challenge to UT-Austin's affirmative action policy, this time to the undergraduate admissions policy, Abigail Fisher was the plaintiff in a lawsuit that contested her rejection to UT-Austin. She alleged that she was not accepted to UT-Austin because of "racial preferences" (Kever 2008, ¶ 1, line 2). The plaintiff's attorneys from the Project on Fair Representation argued that, per *Grutter*, UT-Austin could use affirmative action only if race-neutral alternatives did not succeed in admitting a diverse student body. At UT-Austin, 75 percent of the available places for freshmen go to Texans who graduated in the top 10 percent of their high school classes. The remaining 25 percent of places are decided through individualized application review, in which race and ethnicity may be considered as qualifying factors. The Fifth Circuit Court of Appeals unanimously ruled in favor of the University of Texas in 2011, saying that the admissions policy was in keeping with what the US Supreme Court allowed in *Grutter*. Fisher then appealed that decision to the US Supreme Court.

The court heard the case in 2012 and on June 24, 2013 ruled, 7–1, that institutions of higher education are permitted to consider race and ethnicity as one factor in the admissions process. Justice Elena Kagan had recused herself from the case due to previous involvement. Importantly, the court also remanded the case back to the Fifth Circuit, instructing the court of appeals to address the issue of strict scrutiny, that is, to examine UT-Austin's policy more closely to determine specifically whether the UT-Austin undergraduate admissions policy was indeed narrowly tailored to its goal, as laid out in *Grutter*. In the majority opinion, Justice Anthony Kennedy wrote, "Strict scrutiny does not permit a court to accept a school's assertion that its admission process uses race in a permissible way without closely examining how the process works in practice, yet that is what the District Court and Fifth Circuit did here" (Supreme Court of the United States 2013, 12). What this means for affirmative action policy is that the court declined to strike down the *Grutter* precedent through *Fisher*. However, at the time of this writing, the Supreme Court has elected to hear the *Fisher* case again during the 2015–2016 session.

Once again, the US Supreme Court reaffirmed the *Grutter* and *Bakke* precedents that highlight the ideal of diversity and allow institutions of higher education to consider race and ethnicity in admissions processes. Nevertheless, efforts at the state level have been undermining and continue to undermine affirmative action, due to discordant understandings of what the ideals of equality and liberty require of education policy.

State Bans of Affirmative Action

> The state shall not discriminate against, or grant preferential treatment to, any individual or group on the basis of race, sex, color, ethnicity, or national origin in the operation of public employment, public education, or public contracting.

The above language formed the primary text of most of the state ballot initiatives seeking to curb the use of affirmative action in public institutions.[9] Anti-affirmative action initiatives have passed in six states: California (1996), Washington (1998), Michigan (2006), Nebraska (2008), Arizona (2010), and Oklahoma (2012).[10] Similar ballot initiatives were proposed in two other states: Colorado and Missouri. In Missouri the initiative did not make it onto the ballot despite three attempts. Perhaps the most interesting development was in Colorado where the initiative was on the ballot but was defeated by a narrow margin. And in two additional states, affirmative action has been eliminated due to a governor's executive order (*viz.*, Florida, 2000) or a law passed in the state legislature (*viz.*, New Hampshire, 2012). In this section I examine the key pieces of state legislation in California, Michigan, and Colorado.

California's Proposition 209

Spurred on by then-University of California (UC) Regent Ward Connerly, who holds libertarian views about equality and who situates himself within the color-blind paradigm (Connerly 2000), in 1995 the UC Regents voted to bar the consideration of race and ethnicity in admissions decisions in the UC system by approving system guideline SP-1.[11] California's Proposition 209 soon followed. Known by proponents as the California Civil Rights Initiative (CCRI), Proposition 209 was a ballot initiative for a constitutional amendment to abolish all "preferences" based on race, ethnicity, and sex.[12] Even though the proposition never mentioned affirmative action by name, its effect was to eliminate affirmative action in higher education admissions (as well as in other state programs). The impact on California's public college student population was felt almost immediately and is visible to this day. In fall 1998, the flagship UC campus, Berkeley, reported a 52 percent decrease in the number of black and Hispanic first-year students for the first class admitted without affirmative action. Because of this, black and Hispanic students made up only 9.9 percent of the first-year class, well below the 20.7 percent of first-year enrollees the previous year (Healy 1998). At Berkeley's law school, there was only one black student in the entering class of 1997–98. In partial response to the negative attention given to the UC system, in 2001 the Regents voted to rescind their ban on affirmative action (Schevitz 2001). Because of Proposition 209, however, the Regents' change of heart was symbolic and did little to stem the rollback of students of color in the UC system, especially the most selective campuses. Frances Contreras (2005) examined the effects of Proposition 209 on college access at three UC campuses: Los Angeles, Davis, and Riverside. Using *parity* as a measure of access (a ratio comparing admissions rates to proportional representation in the K–12 system), Contreras found that although this ratio did not change for Asian American and white students, significant declines were experienced by African American, Chicano, and Latino students. That is, she found significant underrepresentation of these groups at all three campuses studied. Further, consider that UCLA's first-year class in fall 1997 had 221 African American students; by fall 2006, it included fewer than half that amount—100 (Leonhardt 2007, 78). Research consistently has shown that Proposition 209 has not only degraded equality of educational opportunity for underrepresented minority students at the most selective UC campuses but also had negative effects on the campus climate for students in general and students of color in particular (Backes 2012; Hinrichs 2012; Kidder 2012; Moses, Yun, and Marin 2009).

Michigan's Proposal 2

The political campaign for Proposal 2, once again spearheaded by Connerly and his American Civil Rights Institute, was announced the day that the US Supreme Court issued its decisions in the University of Michigan cases. Although it did not garner enough petition signatures to make it onto the ballot in 2004, two years later Proposal 2 passed with 58 percent of the vote. Immediately following the implementation of Proposal 2, both the University of Michigan and Michigan State University reported decreased percentages in freshmen of color for fall 2007 (Baker 2007). By fall 2009, the University of Michigan's enrollment of African American, Latino/a, and Native American first-year undergraduates decreased from 12.6 percent of the class before the state affirmative action ban to 9.1 percent, even as its overall numbers of applications and enrollment increased (Schultz 2008). Higher education officials in Michigan noted their struggle to conduct admissions and still keep diversity in mind under the constraints of Proposal 2. As Wayne State University Law School Dean Frank Wu explained,

> What do we do if we're serious about racial integration, diversity and the competitiveness of this nation in a global economy? What Prop 2 did was eliminate one method of dealing with these issues, but it doesn't take away the urgency of the issue. (quoted in Erb 2007, ¶ 5)

Research on the public discussion during the campaign surrounding Proposal 2 showed that media coverage on the issue was superficial at best and deceptive at worst (Moses and Saenz 2008). Neither relevant moral and political issues nor research evidence were presented to voters, resulting in an important state decision made without sufficient dialogue or attempts at understanding the nature of the dispute. I turn next to the initiative campaign in Colorado, which had a different outcome.

Colorado's Amendment 46

Two states had ultimately unsuccessful state ballot initiative proposals for November 2008—Colorado and Missouri. Some commentators pointed out that the timing of these initiative campaigns was strategic, with the aim of capitalizing on the immigration debates and influencing the outcome of the presidential election (Bello 2007).

In Missouri, the initiative never made it onto the ballot. Colorado's case is particularly interesting. Amendment 46 was defeated by a narrow margin: 50.7 percent against and 49.2 percent in favor (Denverpost.com 2008). During the campaign, sponsors of Amendment 46 collected more than 128,000 petition signatures, well more than the 76,047 valid signatures needed to get the initiative on the ballot (Gandy 2008). As in other targeted states, Colorado has relatively few students of color at its state colleges and universities, with about 72 percent of its 2005 first-time, degree-seeking college enrollment identifying as white (Moses, Yun, and Marin 2009). This is especially true of the flagship institution of the University of Colorado Boulder, where in 2005, only 1.4 percent of first-time, degree-seeking college students were African American, 6.3 percent Latino, and 6.5 percent Asian American (Moses, Yun, and Marin 2009). The defeat of Amendment 46 in Colorado marked the first time such an initiative failed to pass at the state level. Several proposed theories explain why Coloradans voted to defeat Amendment 46, including the governor's public opposition to the measure, President Obama's strong support in Colorado, the state's large Latino population, the confusing language of the ballot initiative, an unprecedented grassroots effort against it, television and radio advertisements, and a state ballot that included thirteen other ballot measures. A study of voter beliefs and attitudes about Amendment 46 and affirmative action in Colorado found that misperceptions and misunderstandings about the intent and consequences of the initiative itself played a part in how citizen voted (Moses et al. 2010). Yet opportunities for dialogue and deliberation about affirmative action prior to the election contributed to greater information and understanding, which I explore in chapter 5. First I explore the moral and political roots of the disagreement about affirmative action and other race-conscious education policies aiming to foster greater opportunities for students of color. The central puzzle here, as I see it, is how it is that people disagree despite agreement on basic moral values. We agree about the importance of equality, yet disagree about whether affirmative action promotes greater equality or inequality. The next chapter delves into this controversy.

THREE

The Nature of Moral Disagreement

Conflicting Ideals?

> In the main, this controversy [affirmative action] does not turn on the facts, and it will not be resolved by more or better evidence.
>
> —Glenn Loury 2002, 131

Here Loury is getting at a crucial component of moral disagreement: it resists resolution based on facts or empirical observations and instead is characterized by nuances of values and beliefs. Before getting more deeply into the nature of moral disagreements in general and the moral disagreement about affirmative action in particular, an example would be instructive. My research team and I studied the factors that influenced people's votes for or against Colorado's anti-affirmative action ballot initiative, Amendment 46 (Moses et al. 2010). What we found demonstrates the power that people's moral values and paradigms had in how they interpreted the language of the ballot initiative. Data from a survey of 507 Colorado voters[1] conducted after Amendment 46 failed at the ballot show that a significant number of people voted the opposite of their intention because they were confused by the language used in the initiative.[2] By and large the voters surveyed agreed that equal opportunity is a paramount democratic ideal, regardless of whether they voted for or against affirmative action. In addition, they agreed with concepts such as civil rights and nondiscrimination. All of these concepts were invoked in the language of Amendment 46. As a result, we found that voters were likely to be mistaken regarding the intent, meaning, and consequences of Amendment 46, and this affected how they voted. A vast majority of voters could not accurately explain the consequences of passing Amendment 46.[3] Perhaps most important, the effects of confusion were magnified for the survey respondents who favored affirmative action and mistakenly believed Amendment 46 would preserve it. So, not only was misunderstanding about the intent of Amendment 46 widespread, it was also directional. Few voters with negative feelings toward affirmative action misunderstood the intent of Amendment 46. Voters with positive attitudes toward affirmative action were more likely not only to misunderstand the intended outcome of the initiative but also to vote for Amendment 46 (which was a vote against affirmative action).

This research highlights the importance of conceptual clarification and understanding in a controversial policy decision about which significant disagreement remains. Of course, it is the nature of a democracy that citizens do not agree on all or even many sociopolitical issues. That is part of the beauty of a democratic system. It accommodates disagreement and dissent. Indeed these can make for lively and rich citizen participation and deliberation within democratic politics. Disagreement, however, also can make for contentious, fractious debate, with stakeholders arguing in combative ways and often talking past each other about issues related to conflicting values and beliefs. What I am most interested in here are such disagreements about education policy issues related to race and ethnicity, civil rights, justice, and fairness. Citizens want policies that they think are just and fair. In arguing for their policy preferences, they tend to invoke—either explicitly or implicitly—the democratic ideals of equality, liberty, and/or diversity. But what they mean by those ideals is highly subject to interpretation, and those interpretations are shaped by moral values and paradigms, as we see with the example of voter confusion about Amendment 46. As I mention in chapter 1, I no longer think that traditional argumentation and debate will lead us to resolution of disagreements about thorny education policy issues like affirmative action. Such philosophical and empirical arguments do provide much-needed information for stakeholders and other members of the public, but they also tend to entrench people's policy positions (Ryfe 2005; Schkade, Sunstein, and Hastie 2006). I am interested in shifting scholars' focus from using their policy expertise primarily for theory building and argumentation to using their expertise in and with the community in opportunities for dialogue and deliberation. Ultimately, I argue that an important and effective way to reach just policy compromises is for us to talk about our disagreements and learn to understand the nature of the disagreements. Such dialogue is potentially transformative; participants question their own beliefs as well as the beliefs of others (Graves 2013). Often this leads to more expansive and equitable views (Mezirow 2000).

The purpose of this chapter, then, is to examine the moral and political roots of education policy disagreements. I first examine just what a *moral* disagreement is and make the case that affirmative action ought to be seen as a moral disagreement. I then argue that understanding the nature of moral disagreement enriches the discussion of specific policy controversies that have implications for the ethical treatment of students. As I note in chapters 1 and 2, I use the affirmative action debate as a case example of an enduring moral disagreement, though my larger argument certainly has implications for other controversial education policies. To clarify the terms of the moral disagreement over affirmative action, I analyze how the broad political theories of justice that dominate the debate—egalitarian political theory and libertarian political theory—interpret the moral ideals of equality and liberty, and how those theories interact with the ideas of race egalitarianism and color blindness. I then examine the relationship between moral disagreement and education policy, paying close attention to why understanding and addressing moral disagreement over education policy is important. I endeavor to show how key political and moral ideals may be understood by members of opposing groups, using the most prominent justifications for affirmative action as illustrative of the different ways of thinking about possible common ground.

Context for Moral Disagreement

In 1978, in upholding the constitutionality of race-conscious affirmative action, US Supreme Court Justice Harry Blackmun explained, "In order to get beyond racism, we must first take account of race. There is no other way. And in order to treat some persons equally, we must treat them differently" (*Regents of the University of California* 1978, 407). Nearly thirty years later, the court ruled against race-conscious student assignment policies, with Chief Justice John Roberts writing in his majority opinion: "The way to stop discrimination on the basis of race is to stop discriminating on the basis of race" (*Parents Involved in Community Schools* 2007, 40–41).

The Blackmun–Roberts disagreement highlights that Americans cannot agree about affirmative action. The public conversation is laden with contradictions regarding issues of race-conscious education policy and equality of educational opportunity. Consider that the suite of affirmative action–related US Supreme Court decisions in *Regents of the University of California v. Bakke* (1978) and—twenty-five years later—in *Gratz v. Bollinger* and *Grutter v. Bollinger* (2003), as well as its most recent rulings in *Fisher v. University of Texas* (2013) and *Schuette v. Coalition to Defend Affirmative Action* (2014) have not served to quell the public debate even as they *have* served to support the constitutionality of and provide the strict legal contours for affirmative action in higher education admissions. For proponents of the importance of diversity in fostering a rich and meaningful educational experience, the Supreme Court's landmark decision in *Grutter* came as a relief. The court directly addressed the question of whether colleges and universities could legally consider race and ethnicity in their admissions processes. Any relief, however, was short lived.

Indeed, just four years after the *Gratz* and *Grutter* decisions, a newly comprised high court ruled against the voluntary K–12 race-conscious student assignment plans in Louisville, Kentucky, and Seattle, Washington. Political candidates and appointees also waffle on issues related to affirmative action, not wanting to alienate potential supporters. Individual universities curb affirmative action and related race-conscious programs even as they call for increased diversity on campus. And voters in California, Washington, Michigan, Nebraska, Arizona, and Oklahoma have approved state ballot initiatives identical (or very similar) to Amendment 46, which effectively abolish affirmative action programs. In Michigan this occurred even after the state's flagship university invested substantial resources defending affirmative action in front of the US Supreme Court. What is going on here? The disagreement about affirmative action must be more profound than we currently understand it to be. It cannot be simply about access to higher education, or racism, or discrimination. It is, of course, about those things, but it is also—importantly, I argue—a *moral* disagreement. That is, the affirmative action debate is an example of an enduring moral disagreement, one that arouses profound conflict over fundamental moral ideals such as equality, liberty, and diversity.

This conflict of ideals is exemplified by the Blackmun–Roberts disagreement. The ideas put forward by Justices Blackmun and Roberts represent two opposing moral paradigms related to race in the United States: race egalitarianism and color blindness (Loury 2002; Moses 2011). These moral paradigms underlie one's stance on affirmative action or other such policy initiatives to foster social equality. Supporters of race egalitarianism believe, like Justice Blackmun, that the past and present racism and inequality in the United States compels the state to allow race consciousness in public policies related to educational and employment opportunities (Loury 2002). By contrast, supporters of color blindness believe, like Justice Roberts, that it is pernicious to individual liberty to account for race through public policy. In part, Chief Justice Roberts used the logic of the *Brown v. Board of Education of Topeka* decision to justify his opinion that any use of race in assigning K–12 students constitutes an illegal form of discrimination (*Parents Involved in Community Schools* 2007, 746–48). These opposing worldviews lead not only to heated debates over race consciousness but also to very different policy prescriptions (Lakoff 2002). And they stem from deeper theories of justice based in liberal egalitarian and libertarian political philosophies. I make the case in this chapter that both proponents and opponents of race-conscious admissions policies claim to value the ideal of equality. Similarly, each supports the ideals of liberty and diversity as well (see, e.g., amicus curiae briefs in the Michigan cases by American Council on Education 2003 and United States 2003). Although both egalitarian and libertarian theories of justice embrace these values (equality and liberty), each one gives one of the two values precedence and allows the definition of one to shape the other (i.e., equality circumscribes liberty for egalitarians, and libertarians believe that the greatest way to recognize equality among people is to provide the greatest freedom for those people). A central question thus emerges: how is it that those on either side of the affirmative action debate share significant moral ideals yet endorse opposing policy prescriptions? In a related vein, is there space within a deliberative democracy for intractable policy disagreement? How are important ideals like equality and liberty conceptualized within the political debate? As citizens increasingly participate in decision making about race-conscious education policy, how do scholars and experts fit into public discussion and democratic deliberation? These questions guide the inquiry in the book, and this chapter provides the theoretical and conceptual framing for answering these questions.

Defining Moral Disagreement

What is moral disagreement? How is it important for examining the case of affirmative action policy?

Fittingly for an analysis on disagreement, there is no easy agreement among theorists as to what exactly constitutes a *moral* disagreement. There is even little agreement on what such disagreements ought to be called; the terms *radical moral disagreement, partial moral disagreement, moral conflict, intractable controversy, internal moral disagreement, irreconcilable moral disagreement, reasonable disagreement,* and so on are all present within the scholarly literature.

So what makes a particular disagreement a moral one? Moral disagreements concern enduring, contested public issues involving values, relationships, and ideals, as opposed to individual, personal disputes. There can certainly be personal disputes embedded in larger moral disagreements, but disagreements become moral ones when they center on public issues with broad social consequences. Moral disagreements are qualitatively different from disagreements based on factual issues or differences of opinion, taste, or style. After a fender-bender, two people may disagree over whose car reached the stop sign first, or as baseball fans they may disagree about whether to root for the Mets or the Yankees. These are not moral disagreements. But if two people disagree or two political perspectives conflict about the state's role in providing public aid for people living in poverty, this *is* likely a moral disagreement. For at root this is a disagreement over what priority should be given to the fundamental moral ideals of equality and liberty in a democratic society such as that of the United States. Moral disagreements are based largely on the conceptual schemes and theories of justice that underlie people's views.

Moral disagreements endure despite significant agreement about factual and even moral considerations. Disputants may agree about factual claims and (some) moral values, but disagree in their moral evaluations (i.e., about what to *do*). So, in the case of race-conscious education policies like affirmative action, there exists a persistent moral disagreement despite ostensible *agreement* about the importance of basic moral ideals such as freedom and equality. Of course, the opposing sides do not agree on all moral ideals. Agreement about moral basics does not mean that there will be the same moral beliefs about certain kinds of cases. For example, those who hold libertarian political theory to be tenable can value equality but believe that affirmative action is not the means to that end, whereas those with a liberal egalitarian perspective may believe that affirmative action is a good mechanism to foster equality. But is there an irreconcilable disagreement—a moral deadlock? Different moral opinions exist, to be sure, as well as different moral priorities. Moral deadlock, Ronald Milo (1986) allows, can be the end result of this type of moral disagreement. It can stem from bad reasoning or conflicting interpretations of shared moral ideals (Nelson 2010). For instance, both liberal egalitarian and libertarian theories of justice, which underlie the main opposing positions in the public moral disagreement over affirmative action, may claim to value the basic moral ideals of liberty and equality. But how each ideal is interpreted and prioritized within these theories of justice differs substantially. In addition, the motives behind the claims can be questioned. Thus is born a persistent moral disagreement despite seemingly shared central moral and political ideals.

Accordingly, Amy Gutmann and Dennis Thompson (1996) call moral disagreement the most formidable challenge to democracy today; they lament that our present democratic system provides no adequate way to cope with fundamental value conflicts. Their answer is to conceive of a democracy that has a central place for moral discussion in political and public life—what they and others call *deliberative democracy*.

Serious debate occurs over policy, but generally scant attention is paid to the moral principles and political commitments that underlie it. Too often this results in an unreflective acceptance of ideas and policies that claim to uphold such principles as if they are uncontroversial. It is difficult to argue against broad and often vague concepts such as justice, equality of opportunity, liberty, and so on. Moral disagreement is possible only when opposing sides substantially agree on what the relevant issues and principles are within the debate (Milo 1986). Otherwise there is no basis for even a conversation, much less mutual understanding or ultimately resolution. Based on these ideas, the debate over affirmative action policy constitutes a moral disagreement, one in which both sides agree about the relevance of the moral and political ideals of equality and liberty. There is, at the very least, basis for a conversation, one that may lead to better understanding.

The Roots of the Disagreement: Moral Ideals and Political Commitments

I argue, then, that illuminating the moral and political roots of the disagreement over affirmative action is important for gaining a more profound understanding of how to best inform public discussion of such race-conscious policies. That said, the long-standing disagreement over affirmative action has its roots in other factors as well, not the least of which is racism (Feagin 2002). While those social roots have received attention in the scholarly literature (e.g., Bonilla-Silva 2009; Feagin 2002; Feinberg 1998; West 1993; Williams 1991), the political theories of justice that underlie the disagreement have not.

Specific conceptions and political uses of the moral ideals of equality, liberty, and diversity characterize the political commitments central to egalitarian and libertarian theories of justice. With the firm acknowledgment that there is substantial complexity and overlap within and between prominent theories of justice along the political spectrum from the left to the right, I have chosen purposefully to focus this examination on the commitments of egalitarianism and libertarianism. Either explicitly or implicitly, these two theories underlie much practical policy debate in the United States.[4] Egalitarians and libertarians view the democratic ideal of equality differently, so let me lay out the conflicting interpretations of the concept of "equal treatment." The difference stems from the conceptual distinction between being treated *as an equal* and being treated *equally*. To treat a person *as an equal* requires us to recognize the relevant differences in persons' life situations and treating them accordingly in order for the ideal of equality to be served well. By contrast, being treated equally signifies sameness of treatment, regardless of history, context, or social structures (Dworkin 2000; Gutmann 1999). While egalitarians hope policy strives for the former, libertarians aim for the latter (Gutmann 2003; Viteritti 1999).

In the next sections, I clarify what the prominent ideals mean within egalitarian and libertarian theories and how those meanings inform policy views.

Equality

A discussion of equality at a high level of abstraction may be unproblematic regardless of one's underlying theory of justice. All persons are equal under the law, period. It is at a more practical level that meaningful differences arise, especially in interpretation (Rosenfeld 1991).

One strand of egalitarian theory has held that equality is *the* fundamental moral ideal (Dworkin 2000; Kymlicka 1992). Ronald Dworkin (2000) articulates this perspective well and connects the ideal of equality with the concept of equal concern. "Equal concern," he writes, "is the sovereign virtue of political community—without it government is only tyranny—and when a nation's wealth is very unequally distributed, as the wealth of even very prosperous nations now is, then its equal concern is suspect" (1). In order for people to be treated with equal concern, they need to have equality of resources. By resources, Dworkin means something akin to opportunities and possibilities for flourishing. In education policy, this perspective is embodied in policies aiming to foster access to education, such as affirmative action, Title IX, and bilingual education. For a theory of justice to be taken seriously, Dworkin concludes, each person has to matter equally, to be treated as an equal. Of significant note here is that *treatment as an equal* does not necessarily imply getting the *same* treatment.

Another strand of egalitarianism—liberal egalitarianism—follows more closely the work of John Rawls (1971, 1993, 2001) by emphasizing equality of opportunity.[5] Consequently, treatment as an equal requires equality of opportunity. Each person should have a right to equal basic liberties, positions and offices should be open to all under the principle of fair equality of opportunity, and inequality is permissible only so long as any inequalities result in maximizing the position of the worst off, that is, those with the fewest primary goods. Consider public school accommodations for students with disabilities; in a sense the students with disabilities are getting *more* in terms of resources than students without disabilities, but that inequality is justified. For Rawls (1971), persons' talents, abilities, and initial life circumstances are "arbitrary from a moral point of view," and, as such, it is unfair to reward them as if they *deserved* what they drew in the natural and social lotteries (74). Furthermore, his idea of equality requires that any differences of resources benefit the least advantaged.

The concepts of equality and equality of opportunity can be interpreted to mean a variety of quite different and, often, conflicting things. The following examples of think tanks and other popular policy organizations across the political spectrum champion equality of opportunity, but they may or may not be interested in Dworkin's ideal of treating people as equals or Rawls's idea of justice as fairness. Consider the following two advocacy organizations: the Advocacy Center for Equality and Democracy, which aims to foster policies that promote economic equality (i.e., the redistribution of wealth and resources), and the Center for Equal Opportunity, which aims to foster policies that promote color blindness and assimilation. Even though both centers seem to promote the importance of equality as a fundamental value, the use of similar terms can be misleading. Indeed, concepts may be used for political reasons, with little to no regard for what they mean or what they require of social policy.

Nevertheless, it is important to take note of even small glimmers of conceptual agreement. And indeed, there is often agreement within political theories about the principle of *basic* equality—that persons should be treated as equals and that the state ought to treat persons with equal concern and respect (Dworkin 1977; Gutmann 2003). This idea should be unproblematic, yet a conflict comes in defining what *treatment as equals* means. For libertarians, treatment as equals means that we respect a person's property ownership—her or his self as well as her or his material goods. The fact that such a primary principle may result in vast socioeconomic inequality is unproblematic within libertarian political theory, so long as property rights and procedures for the acquisition and transfer of property are fair.

Liberty

Libertarians characterize the moral and political ideal of liberty as "requiring that each person should have the greatest amount of liberty commensurate with the same liberty for all" (Sterba 1992, 5). The role of the state is to protect human rights that are centered on liberty (Starr 2007). John Hospers (1974) names three human rights as central to a libertarian theory of justice: the right to life (to protect people from force and coercion, unjust killing), the right to liberty (to protect freedom of speech, press, assembly, ideas), and the right to property (to protect material and intellectual property from theft, fraud, slander, etc.). Within this understanding of the role of the state, the state is not obligated to provide citizens with assistance, such as public aid, which might promote some persons' welfare.

Often cited as the source for libertarian political theory, Friedrich von Hayek (1960, 85) argues that the libertarian ideal of liberty is characterized by two primary tenets: (1) "equality before the law" as "the only kind of equality conducive to liberty and the only equality which we can secure without destroying liberty" rather than "substantial equality" and (2) "reward according to perceived value" rather than "reward according to merit." As a result, inequalities caused by the luck of birth circumstances and talent are seen as just.

Robert Nozick (1974), long held up as the representative of libertarian political philosophy,[6] puts forward a libertarian theory of justice as "entitlement," characterized by respect for rights of ownership of self and property, which allows persons the freedom to choose how they want to live their lives without intrusion by the state. Why should any goods acquired within the free market be redistributed when one's talents, abilities, work ethic, and possessions are one's own?

Libertarianism holds that vast structural inequalities could be just, that is, could come about in a just manner, even though they might be unfortunate. There might be bad luck involved in people's starting places in life, but not necessarily injustice. So long as the state respects the people's property rights and fosters liberty without becoming coercive, then the resulting distribution of goods should be considered just. Likewise, race should play no part in public life; laws and policy should be color blind. As a result, a formalist notion of opportunity (Howe 1997) that calls for merely equal access to education—without official barriers—is considered just.

The libertarian interpretation of liberty does not imply that libertarians do not care whether less advantaged people have their basic needs met; it means that libertarians believe that the state has no duty to provide for those needs. Social welfare is therefore the requirement of charity, not of the state. One example of this idea in practice was the George W. Bush administration's call for faith-based charities and organizations to lead in the provision of social services for people in poverty. Although controversial,[7] this was justified through the belief that under a free market system and a minimal state, the least advantaged would have enough opportunities and resources to make sure that their basic needs are met.

Although egalitarians share the value of liberty, they believe that justice requires equality as the predominant value. Egalitarians hold liberty and autonomy to be important but recognize and emphasize how social structures constrain its exercise (Moses 2002).

Basic Equality as a Shared Ideal

Even though an egalitarian theory of justice considers equality of income or resources to be a prerequisite for treating people as equals and a libertarian theory of justice deems the right to one's own work, effort, and property as a requirement for treating people as equals, both theories invoke the ideal of basic equality. Consider that Will Kymlicka (1992) points out that, traditionally, theorists have believed that a continuum of political theories of justice exists, from the left to the right, and that each of these appeals to a different ultimate foundational value. The theories, therefore, have been seen as incompatible, their differences as incapable of resolution. Kymlicka follows Dworkin in saying that a regard for *basic equality* (characterized not by an equal distribution of income and wealth, but by the more abstract idea of treating people as equals) is what should be viewed as the *ultimate* foundational value held by political theories from the left to the right. The point is that each and every person matters equally, and Kymlicka (1992) notes that "this more basic notion of equality is found in Nozick's libertarianism as much as Marx's communism" (4).

This is a key point. The ideal of basic equality holds an important place in both egalitarian and libertarian political theory. Some educators, researchers, and other policy actors may feel clear about how they interpret and prioritize the moral and political ideals that guide their policy positions. Nevertheless, the ideals and their place in the conceptual schemes that drive positions are often implicit, which makes it difficult for citizens to make informed choices about policy prescriptions. In order to make the most knowledgeable, coherent, and consistent choices, policy actors need to be clear not only about their own moral ideals but also about the moral ideals within opposing views. Of course, no guarantee ensures that a more profound understanding of one's own views as well as the views of one's opponents will lead one to change one's positions on policy issues. Agreement on larger ideals does not necessarily mitigate deep disputes about what the larger agreement requires of policy prescriptions (Waldron 1999). Many factors other than rational deliberation and argument make up conceptual schemes and influence policy views. What is important to take away from the preceding discussion of the moral ideals of equality and liberty and how they function to shape egalitarian and libertarian theories of justice is that, regardless of the motivations, at least some agreement exists over basic ideals. The moral disagreements over policy stem from a combination of contrasting prioritization, interpretation, and application of the salient principles. Within libertarianism, basic equality is perceived as necessary for enhancing liberty. As a result of the different ideas of what liberty and equality involve, justice for libertarians may require laws and policies that conflict with what justice requires for egalitarians. But there is hope. Because there are important similarities in basic moral ideals, deeper understanding of the ideals and how they affect policy controversies may move us toward a theory of justice that can be more widely embraced. The ideal of diversity provides another example.

Diversity

Diversity has become a very visible cultural ideal in the United States, one that holds "a special, almost sacrosanct place in our public discourse" (Schuck 2003a, B10). Both supporters and opponents of affirmative action have expressed support for the ideal of diversity. For example, former president Bill Clinton has said, "Our rich texture of racial, religious and political diversity will be a Godsend in the 21st century" (Clinton 2001, n.p.). Former president George W. Bush has said that he "strongly support[s] diversity of all kinds, including racial diversity in higher education" (Bush 2003, n.p.). Certainly, the term *diversity* itself is contested; it can have various meanings and is quite controversial in that those on both sides of the affirmative action debate may support "diversity." At the most basic level, however, *diversity* means variety or heterogeneity. In discussions centering on affirmative action, people tend to focus on race/ethnicity. For the purpose of this chapter, diversity is characterized by a variety of races, ethnicities, colors, cultures, ages, religions, socioeconomic backgrounds, genders, sexual orientations, gender identities, abilities, languages, and so on. These are qualities people hold that cannot easily be changed. In the context of educational benefits, diversity also includes things that can be changed, such as values, beliefs, moral ideals, intellectual understandings, and political ideologies.

As with the ideals of equality and liberty, there are varying interpretations of the ideal of diversity and what it means for education policy. From a libertarian political perspective, diversity is an ideal with some value, but it problematically has ascended in importance to match the concepts of equality and liberty (Barry 2002; Schuck 2003b; Wood 2003). Peter Wood (2003) especially lauds the ideal of liberty and is concerned that the ideal of diversity not overshadow liberty or equality. Another more practical concern for libertarians is that considering racial diversity in college admissions serves to disadvantage low-income students and students in poverty (Garfield 2006).

Libertarians are particularly concerned that emphasizing the ideal of diversity not derail attempts at national unity. Misunderstanding what proponents of contemporary diversity believe to be real equality, Wood (2003) asserts, "real equality, according to diversicrats, consists of parity among groups, and to achieve it, social goods must be measured out in ethnic quotas, purveyed by group preferences, or otherwise filtered according to the will of social factions" (14). In actuality, as noted earlier, egalitarian proponents of the ideal of diversity—historically and now—understand real equality to be characterized by treatment of people as equals.

According to the libertarian perspective, the ideas that bolster the diversity rationale have trumped an older (and to them, more acceptable) notion of diversity, which emphasized unity forged from multiple identities and assimilation (Barry 2002; Ravitch 1995; Wood 2003). By contrast, they would argue that the contemporary diversity rationale stresses particularity for its own sake, highlighting the group at the expense of the whole. Wood (2003), for example, is concerned that the diversity rationale is founded on the untenable "*belief* that the portion of our individual identity that derives from our ancestry is the most important part, and a *feeling* that group identity is somehow more substantial and powerful than either our individuality or our common humanity" (11). Thus, libertarians do not believe that the ideal of diversity can be used to justify what they deem as special—largely unearned—and divisive privileges for racial and ethnic groups.

Egalitarian theory sees that unity and common humanity can actually be fostered by diversity. The ideas of unity and diversity need not be mutually exclusive; indeed individual and group diversity that is sustained over time can contribute to greater mutual human understanding and respect. Too often the unity for which Wood and similar critics are nostalgic suppressed the very diversity from which it came. Students, as Martha Nussbaum (1997) argues, need to be able to reflect on themselves, their culture, community, and nation—critically—to achieve an education for democracy and world citizenship. Similarly, Philip Green (1998) discusses the idea of "egalitarian solidarity" (186), which is established when democratic participants have certain dispositions such as mutual respect and mutual recognition. As Green explains,

> It is the disposition to ally oneself with others not because they are similar
> to oneself in social background or agree with one's own tastes and values

but precisely because they are different *and yet* have permanently common human interests. It is the mutual recognition of *these* interests, not the mere recognition of being in the same economic or social position, that defines solidarity among equals. Without this sense of mutual recognition, as well as the sentiment of empathy that underlies it, a mass politics of resentment is possible but egalitarian politics is not. (187)

Whereas Green argues for egalitarian solidarity, I argue that dialogue will move us toward being able to stand in others' shoes in such a way that we can reach the promise of egalitarian solidarity. Dialogue cultivates the dispositions necessary for solidarity including understanding, empathy, respect, and recognition.

Understanding the Ideas of Race Egalitarianism and Color Blindness

In understanding that the ideal of equality has defenders and supporters across the political spectrum, it is important to understand also that because race and ethnicity continue to matter in educational and social opportunities, the positive rhetoric around equality and equal educational opportunity needs to be bolstered by deeper understandings about the substance of the ideal. The opposing views on equal treatment examined above are indicative of what Chantal Mouffe (2009) calls a paradox in modern democracy: the conflicting relationship between equality and liberty. Mouffe posits that antagonism "can never be eliminated and it constitutes an ever-present possibility in politics. A key task of democratic politics is therefore to create the conditions that would make it less likely for such a possibility to emerge" (13). As related to issues of race in America, the disagreement about equal treatment also is marked by a systemic avoidance of acknowledging and discussing issues related to race and ethnicity. Consider the trial of George Zimmerman in the killing of black teen Trayvon Martin; race, which seemed a crucial factor in the tragic incident, largely was omitted from the trial, even as social media seemed to focus primarily on issues of race (Yankah 2013). To take a less charged example, consider the phenomenon of whitening a résumé; some young professionals of color feel the need to change their names to more white-sounding names to get job interviews (Luo 2009). Indeed, white-sounding names on résumés receive 50 percent more calls for interviews (Bertrand and Mullainathan 2004).

The election of President Barack Obama served to highlight the conflict between the paradigms of race egalitarianism and color blindness. Both Obama campaigns made conscious and concerted efforts to avoid race-based controversy (Tesler and Sears 2010). As a presidential candidate, Obama walked a delicate line, balancing the need for approval from both white voters and black voters; he could not seem "too Black," but he had to be "Black enough" (Metzler 2010, 401). Although a majority of white voters did not vote for him in 2008, 43 percent of whites did; combined with the large majority of voters of color supporting him, in the end, Obama's political attempt at being a racially unifying candidate succeeded (Brooks 2009; Tesler and Sears 2010). As Shelby Steele (2008) explains, "[Obama] embodies something that no other presidential candidate possibly can: the idealism that race is but a negligible human difference. Here is the racialism, innate to his pedigree, that automatically casts him as the perfect antidote to America's corrosive racial politics" (8). Nevertheless, for all the hope and promise imbued in Obama's election as president, for both race relations and democracy, race theorists remain skeptical of his approach and of the subsequent claims of a new "post-racial" America that has finally transcended its racist past.

The first Obama campaign, however, was not "post-racial." In fact, voters viewed candidate Obama in a racialized way, even though "he was consistently portrayed as the racially transcendent candidate" (Tesler and Sears 2010, 6–7). Of chief concern is that viewing Obama's election as the mark of a "post-racial" era will vitiate important policy efforts aimed at mitigating racial inequality in schools and society, such as efforts to foster racial integration and educational opportunities. Accordingly, Tim Wise (2010) contends that Obama's focus on racial transcendence exemplified color-blind ideology, which could actually serve to worsen racial discrimination. He argues that Obama's election,

> far from serving as evidence that racism had been defeated, might signal a mere shape-shifting of racism, from Racism 1.0 to Racism 2.0, an insidious upgrade that allows millions of whites to cling to racist stereotypes about people of color generally, while nonetheless carving out exceptions for those who, like Obama, make us comfortable by seeming so "different" from what we view as a much less desirable norm. (15)

Such views highlight color blindness in education policy, bolstering reform efforts that aim to be independent of race, as if achievement gaps and segregated schools were no longer racialized issues.

The Relationship between Equal Treatment and Race Egalitarianism

The US Civil Rights Act of 1964 focused on nondiscrimination in reaction to, among other things, blatant and subtle admissions and hiring practices that discriminated against Asian American, black, Latino/a, Native American, and female students and workers (Graham 1990). When the Civil Rights Act aimed to extend equal opportunity to all, regardless of race, ethnicity, or gender, it was within a sociohistorical context of rampant negative discrimination against people of color. At that time, moving toward an ideal of color blindness seemed to be a step forward. The color-blind ideal was complicated and challenged by the idea of using positive discrimination to ensure greater opportunities for people of color and women. Soon after, federal law established policies to compensate for social inequalities based on race, ethnicity, and sex, sanctioning the idea that such minority status could be viewed as what Gutmann (1999) calls "relevant qualifications" for admittance into higher education (197–203). This "qualifications" argument holds that an applicant's race, ethnicity, or gender may be relevant for helping fulfill the social mission of universities, which includes educating professionals and leaders who can serve democracy in general and diverse communities in particular.

Libertarian (and conservative)[8] political theorists contend affirmative action diminishes equality of opportunity for nonbeneficiaries (Connerly 2009; Thernstrom and Thernstrom 1997). This argument stems from a belief that formal equality—that is, the absence of formal and legal barriers to opportunities—is sufficient for an equitable society. Such a contention, however, conflicts with the egalitarian interpretation of equality I described earlier. Consider John Dewey's (1927) interpretation: "Equality does not signify that kind of *mathematical or physical equivalence* in virtue of which any one element may be substituted for another. It denotes effective regard for whatever is distinctive and unique in each, irrespective of physical and psychological inequalities" (150–51, emphasis added). To reiterate a key concept, in a democratic community, the concept of *equal treatment* ought to signify something beyond merely the *same* treatment when members of the population differ in relevant ways (Dworkin 2000; Gutmann 1999). That said, the relevant differences approach to conceptualizing equal treatment, that is, treatment *as equals*, could lead to a slippery slope regarding other controversial policies, such as racial profiling. One could argue that skin color is a relevant difference in crime or airline terrorism, and that this justifies not treating all people the same in, say, police investigations or airport security checks.

Putting aside the complex issue of racial profiling as well beyond the scope of this discussion, the difference between using race and ethnicity in higher education admissions and in crime investigation or prevention is the difference between positive discrimination and negative discrimination. Positive discrimination in favor of historically underrepresented groups is permissible by democratic standards; negative discrimination most likely is not (Gutmann 1999). Perhaps more salient is that the two issues are not parallel. In the case of affirmative action, race is viewed and used as a qualification for university study, a good distributed according to merit. Merit here is meant to reflect Gutmann's (1999) idea that a number of things can qualify an applicant for admission into an institution of higher education, and these go beyond the narrow focus on academic qualifications such as grade point average and college entrance examination score.

Yet opponents of race consciousness who follow a color-blind paradigm in the libertarian tradition, like Connerly (2000, 2009), interpret the concepts of equal treatment, equality, and equal rights using a formalist conception of equality and equality of opportunity. In this school of thought, the notion of equal treatment always means *same* treatment, without regard to social structures, context, and past or present discrimination. From this view, in Connerly's (2009) words, affirmative action policies have gone "beyond the level of equal treatment" and "reduced . . . the rights of non-minorities and males" (106). Furthermore, Connerly understands civil rights policies as having "suspended the constitutional guarantee of equal protection for some citizens, particularly whites, in the interest of compensating blacks because their civil rights had been denied for many years" (108), instead of understanding them as providing one policy mechanism to mitigate race and gender-based inequalities. The latter solution recognizes relevant differences related to race, ethnicity, and gender; Connerly's conception does not. Because of these interpretations, Connerly views affirmative action as "preferential treatment"—anathema to the Civil Rights Act—and campaigns for anti-affirmative action ballot initiatives "to restore the principle of equal treatment for all" (109). He sees this principle resting "at the core of American democracy" (111). While egalitarians agree with Connerly that equal treatment is at the core of our democracy, they have very different ways of arriving at "equal treatment for all." The recognition of relevant differences requires a more sophisticated model than the formalist notion of equal treatment as *same* treatment can provide.

Given the rampant social inequalities in the United States, formal notions of nondiscrimination actually can perpetuate oppression against disfavored groups (Anderson 2010; Howe 1997; Young 1990). Gutmann

(1999) calls this "repressive nondiscrimination" (114), meaning that passive nondiscrimination risks repressing democratic deliberation and other social functions of higher education. Iris Marion Young (1990) argues that affirmative action challenges passive nondiscrimination of minority groups. She contends that "if [positive] discrimination serves the purpose of undermining the oppression of a group, it may be not only permitted, but morally required" (197).

Why Understanding Moral Disagreement Matters for Education Policy

As the previous section on the conflict between the paradigms of race egalitarianism and color blindness demonstrates, it is often difficult to ascertain what morality and justice require. This is especially true in issues of education policy. How do we make sense of competing views on policy issues that carry vast significance for students? Is it possible that the conflicting sides can each be right? What does that mean for education policy decisions? Typically, there will be some fallout for making morally controversial decisions—perhaps even some type of moral wrongdoing. Regardless of this, moral disagreement can serve to move people—and society—forward. One need only think of the landmark Supreme Court decisions in *Brown v. Board of Education* and *Roe v. Wade* to understand how moral disagreements can serve as catalysts for social change, however imperfectly implemented that change might be. The point is, moral disagreement can be positive, so long as we are willing to work to understand reasonable opposing views, with mutual respect. A deeper understanding of contested moral ideals and interpretations will illuminate the theory of justice that underlies the policy.

I now consider three prominent objections to the idea that understanding moral disagreement can do any work in addressing difficult policy controversies: the appeal to self-interest, the salience of power and politics, and the assertion of impossibility.

The Self-Interest Objection

The gist of this objection is as follows: Why does understanding moral disagreement matter if in the end human behavior (especially in political matters) is based primarily on self-interest?[9] The point here is that if, all things considered, political choices are made so as to bring about preferred personal outcomes, no amount of increased understanding of one's own and others' moral ideals and theories of justice will matter in practice. Race egalitarians and advocates of color blindness currently seem to be at such an impasse in the United States.

The self-interest explanation for human action stems from Thomas Hobbes's ([1651] 1994) idea that conflict was a defining feature of society. Conflicts arise due to peoples' self-interested nature. Consequently, there is a prominent view that policymaking beliefs and behavior may be based on (a narrow view of) self-interest, a view that is indicative of what Jane Mansbridge (1990) called the "adversary paradigm" of democracy, but this explanation alone cannot account for how education policy decisions are made (10). The narrow view of self-interest holds that rational actors are motivated to do what will benefit them personally, regardless of the consequences for others. Such a narrow view discounts the relational nature of people's moral understandings and actions (Noddings 1984; Walker 1997). We need a more complex view that considers other prominent motivating factors such as moral values, obligation, love, justice, meanness, relationship, and partisanship (Mansbridge 1990). This is not to say that self-interest is not an important factor or that people always care about the welfare of others or the public good. Rather, the way that policy decisions are made is more likely to include some form of self-interest *as well as* other factors based on people's moral values and relationships. Of course, these can be seen as self-interest still, but the notion of self-interest then becomes much broader.

Studies of human behavior reveal motivating factors including the broader idea of self-interest and less putatively "rational" ones such as love and meanness. David Sears and Carolyn Funk's (1990) survey data showed that on certain issues, self-interest is a less powerful motivator than political principles. This explains how, for example, a parent might oppose ability tracking in schools even though such tracking practices would allow her child to be advantaged by being placed in a college preparatory academic track. Similarly, other theories include Robert Frank's (1990) idea for a "commitment model" of action, within which actors may act in a prima facie irrational way due to emotional dispositions and moral commitments (80). And Margaret Urban Walker's (1997) feminist perspective emphasized the collaborative nature of morality, such that moral understandings reflect persons' identities and relationships as well as their own individual interests. These alternative explanations connect with self-interest (rather than refute it completely).

The appeal to self-interest as *the* motivating factor for human action is incomplete. It does not describe the whole of political action on moral issues or take into account how self-interest may change over time. Politicians and policymakers do not only do whatever they need to do just to gain power or political advantage or get elected. Because of the way the US political system works, such narrowly defined self-interested action surely occurs some of the time. But concerning the nature of moral disagreement, it is sometimes unclear whose interests which outcome would serve. Fostering greater understanding of the moral ideals and political commitments embedded in such disagreements pushes us beyond narrow self-interest claims.

The Power and Politics Objection

Expanding on the narrow self-interest objection, the power and politics objection is based on the idea that power and politics alone drive the invocation, interpretation, and use of moral ideals in policy processes. Among other reasons, this objection may stem from the idea that policy processes are more political than rational (Stone 2002) or from an understanding of the policymaking process as a "political spectacle" that is less about democracy and moral ideals and more about gaining political advantage and power (Edelman 1988; Smith et al. 2004). It may also stem from a cynical view of political processes. The general idea here is that moral disagreements over education policy and the concepts and ideals involved can never be taken at face value, especially when race and class are at issue. Powerful forces strategically invoke certain moral ideals to further their political agendas, with little regard for issues of justice or for the least-advantaged persons. For example, the Center for Equal Opportunity has used (some would say co-opted) the language of civil rights to argue against race-conscious education policies, the very policies developed during the civil rights movement to further civil rights, diversity, and equality. The use of the phrase *equal opportunity* may be strategic; it allows the Center to position its work on the moral high ground. No amount of understanding of the nature of moral disagreement can mitigate the strategic political maneuvering surrounding controversial policies, or so the objection goes.

Although issues of power certainly lurk beneath the surface of moral-political debates such as the ones discussed in this chapter and it is fascinating to examine how power and politics affect the language and concepts used by policy actors, it would be unproductive to respond by merely throwing up one's hands and saying that the ideal of equality is sometimes invoked for purely strategic political purposes rather than for any real concern for equality. It would be far more constructive to try to understand how each side conceptualizes equality and try to capitalize on what common ground there is. People may support whatever moral ideals they believe will keep them in power or give them political advantage, but once a moral ideal like equality is used, careful analysis may illuminate the political theories underlying political positions as well as help uncover deeper reasons for its use within particular political theories of justice. Consider that the George W. Bush administration's amicus curiae brief to the Supreme Court in *Grutter v. Bollinger* cited diversity as a desirable characteristic of a strong democratic state, yet urged the court to strike down affirmative action in higher education admissions. We could attribute this support of diversity to disingenuous use of the concept of diversity to seem sympathetic to voters of color. That is certainly one viable interpretation. However, I argue that it is important to go further, to endeavor to understand the seeming agreement between egalitarians and libertarians about diversity in this case, to make sense of the subsequent disagreement over affirmative action policy. At the very least, clarity of meaning and interpretation can serve to highlight the importance of moral ideals like equality and diversity and delineate what they require of public policy. Furthermore, having an understanding of the moral disagreements limits the ability of actors to engage in purely political maneuvering, as language cannot merely be co-opted because the use of that language is likely to be interrogated as part of understanding the moral disagreement.

The Impossibility Objection

A third objection to the importance of understanding the principles, ideals, and theories that drive moral disagreement is the idea that a number of moral disagreements are, simply stated, impossible to resolve. That is, each disputing side may be right in some important way, or any decision or outcome would lead to some moral wrongdoing, or opposing parties will just never be able to agree. So what good does it do to try to understand such disagreements, if there is no hope for satisfactory resolution on the horizon?

This is a very sobering objection, especially because there seem to be myriad examples of moral conflicts that are impossible in some sense. Consider the abortion and euthanasia debates, competing claims about the state's responsibility to people in poverty or undocumented workers; the list could go on. Should we, then, make no final judgments? Where would that get us? How would we address practical issues of education policy that affect the lives of people and educational institutions? Indeed, there may be no one morally best answer in such moral disagreements over policy. That may yet mean, however, that some policy decisions are better than others

(Gowans 1987). And, in some cases, there indeed may be a morally best decision.

The impossibility objection can lead to three related conclusions: moral relativism, inescapable wrongdoing, and irreconcilable worldviews. This strand of argument for moral relativism goes like this: when faced with a moral disagreement that seems irreconcilable, theoretical and practical considerations will lead to moral relativism. That is, if disputing parties cannot reach mutually an acceptable resolution, then they must accept that one particular answer may be correct for one side whereas a different answer may be correct for the other side (Nelson 2010). If the sides cannot agree, then they cannot judge each other either.

Believing it to be an inevitable response to a society rife with difficult moral disagreements, David Wong (1991) characterizes relativism as a "common response to the deepest conflict we face in our ethical lives" (442). Within this view, the opposing sides in such conflicts each may be right; or perhaps their views are not as inconsistent as first they appeared. On the other side, Nicholas Sturgeon (1994) argues that although moral relativism is a possible response to moral disagreement, it does not make sense. According to the anti-relativist position, opposing views can be understandable and even right about subsidiary points, but both cannot be morally *right* on the whole.

I do not aim to solve the issue of objective versus subjective truth herein. Nevertheless, the discussion about relativism is instructive. Does the existence of difficult—even intractable—moral disagreement necessarily point us toward relativism? On the contrary, just because a moral disagreement is difficult to resolve does not mean that ultimately no right answer is possible (George 1999). An illuminating example in support of this conclusion is the US Supreme Court's separate but equal doctrine that held that racial segregation in the United States was legally permissible. The moral disagreement surrounding the issue of legal racial segregation adjudicated in *Brown v. Board of Education* seemed irreconcilable, with each disputing side certain of the moral rectitude of its position. In hindsight, I believe there was *one* morally correct answer: racial segregation is morally wrong because one race is deemed inferior to another, regardless of whether the separate facilities are equal. As Robert George posits, "Even reasonable disagreement does not indicate an absence of objective truth" (186). This is not to say that widespread social agreement about the moral wrongness of racial segregation in theory has resulted in integrated schools and communities in practice. Yet critics of the *Brown* legacy and other civil rights era policies challenge that promise based on evidence from history. Christopher Metzler (2010), for one, maintains:

> For all the good that *Brown*, the Civil Rights Act, and the Voting Rights Act did,
> they did an equal amount of harm. . . . *Brown* ensured that Black children and
> White children could be in the same classroom, but it did nothing to ensure
> that their opportunities for learning would be equal. (397)

Similarly, Derrick Bell (2004) calls *Brown* "a magnificent mirage, the legal equivalent of that city on a hill to which all aspire without any serious thought that it will ever be attained" (4). Indeed, there is significant evidence of the resegregation of schools and communities, about which little is being done (Anderson 2010; Orfield and Frankenberg 2012).

So we see that even if there is a morally best solution, it does not mean that no moral wrongdoing will occur. Indeed, in difficult issues of moral disagreement, regardless of the resolution, moral wrongdoing may occur more often than expected (Gowans 1994). Libertarian advocates of color blindness in education policy argue that students' race or ethnicity do not necessarily influence their educational opportunities; it is internal and cultural factors that may keep students of color from achieving to their potential (Brooks 2009, 1). As such, race-conscious policies actually may be counterproductive to the success of students of color in schools and universities. By contrast, supporters of race-egalitarian policies point to social structures and systems that were created with only white students in mind and that continue to exclude and oppress students of color (Howe 1997).

To consider another example, take the educational practice of ability tracking. In an effort to provide properly challenging curricula and educational experiences for high-achieving students, students often are tracked into classes based largely on their scores on standardized tests. Considerable research has shown this to be a practice that, even though it may indeed benefit those students placed in the highest tracks, invariably harms the students placed in the lowest tracks (Lucas 1999; Oakes 1986). This type of outcome may result in inescapable moral wrongdoing and even moral tragedy (Gowans 1994). If a moral harm occurs as a result of doing something good, there still needs to be moral responsibility for the harm or wrongdoing. Going back to the example of affirmative action, is it a moral wrong to consider race and ethnicity in college and university admissions decisions? Libertarian proponents of color blindness would say yes. This is a complex question that I have taken up in significant detail elsewhere (Moses 2001, 2002). Although the affirmative action debate is a significant moral disagreement, there is promise of a satisfactory resolution that serves to minimize moral harm. Sacrifices will undoubtedly need to be made by each disputing side, but there is no moral tragedy in those sacrifices. In *Grut-*

ter, the Supreme Court ruled that using race as one qualifying factor among many in college and university admissions serves the interests of individual students, individual institutional missions, and the larger public good. A diverse student body is not only beneficial for all students but also for the broader leadership interests of American society. The idea that some moral wrongdoing *may* occur in disputes such as the ones over affirmative action or ability tracking should not cause us to view them as impossible. Severe moral wrongdoing, or moral tragedy, in these types of case is not necessarily inescapable.

The final argument for the impossibility of resolving serious moral disagreements is based on irreconcilable worldviews. It centers on George Lakoff's (2002) argument that impossible conflicts underscore that the major political division within everyday political discourse in the United States—between those he calls liberals and those he calls conservatives (in the popular politics sense rather than the political philosophy sense)—is at bottom a moral one, based on core personal and family values. Lakoff posits that the main ideals are strictness (on the right) and nurturance (on the left), that these values are fundamentally opposed, and that all social and political debates reflect that one major, deep difference. An important consequence is that many moral differences between the two groups may be irreconcilable.

As I have attempted to illustrate, egalitarians and libertarians share some important basic commonalities and values. Lakoff (dis)misses these. Through discourse analysis, he highlights the similarity of the metaphors used for moral issues, but does not consider that those similar metaphors might have their roots in certain shared moral ideals. As such, Lakoff is too quick to point out only the moral differences that lead to divergent worldviews and irresolvable policy disputes.

Compromises about moral disagreements may emerge through different means: (a) moral argumentation (deliberative argument and discussion); (b) empirical discoveries (e.g., scientific discoveries about fetuses or second language acquisition); and (c) educational, cultural, or experiential influences (e.g., when a student leaves home believing that affirmative action is wrong but then in college is exposed to diversity, etc., and changes her or his view) (Silver 1994). The existence of difficult, intractable moral disagreements need not imply that disputants have divergent worldviews that *cannot* be better understood and perhaps overcome. George (1999) makes a cogent point: "To say that a moral question is difficult . . . is in no way to suggest that it admits of no right answer" (186). Indeed, I have argued elsewhere for what I believe to be the "right answer" about affirmative action (Moses 2002, 2010; Moses and Marin 2006), but my argument herein strives to get beyond that to make a larger point about such moral disagreements.

Implications for Education Policy

I have made a case for the importance of understanding the connection between moral disagreement and education policy. I have attempted to present a new way (appeal to moral disagreement) of examining an old problem (education policy controversies). Because so very many controversial education policy issues need deeper theoretical understanding, greater attention to moral disagreement is in order. Education policy processes are sometimes viewed as rational endeavors, with evidence weighed on each side and then a decision made. More often than not, underneath debates over complex education policy issues like affirmative action lie moral disagreements and fears of moral wrongdoing to one side or the other.

In the case of affirmative action policy and race consciousness in education policy, the source of disagreement is not only about disputants' opposing moral values but also about the combination of a difference over the applicability of a commonly held principle requiring equality of educational opportunity and over the priority given to another shared moral principle requiring the protection of individual liberty. Beginning in the 1960s, the federal government's civil rights programs reflected an egalitarian perspective on addressing discrimination and inequality. As chapter 1 explains, this means that equality was seen as a central democratic ideal. Social policies thus reflected a focus on that ideal. For example, after the Bilingual Education Act passed in 1968, programs for English language learners began to be put in place so that emerging bilingual students could learn other subjects as they were learning English. As a result, they could have equality of educational opportunity even though this often meant increased spending on what was then a small student population. Subsequent decades brought significant backlash against this way of justifying equal opportunity policies.

As the case of affirmative action exemplifies, there are different ways of justifying affirmative action and other race-conscious education policies that can appeal to either egalitarian or libertarian ideals separately or both combined. In the section that follows, I identify and examine four prominent justifications for affirmative action that have emerged—remediation, economics, diversity, and social justice—paying special attention to how these exemplify the conflicting ideals discussed in this chapter thus far.

Prominent Justifications for Affirmative Action

US society has been built on the ideal of a democratic government that can use policy to mitigate social and economic inequalities, yet this is challenged by its image as the nation of freedom, where government is neutral and does not impose certain values on its citizens (Moses 2004). In the fifty-year history of affirmative action policy in the United States, we can see that the country has struggled to balance its sometimes-competing moral ideals of equality and liberty (Dworkin 2000). Four prominent justifications for affirmative action illustrate the salience of these moral ideals in that they combine aspects from both egalitarian and libertarian theory. My hope in analyzing the justifications is that we can gain some understanding about how such justificatory emphases could serve to promote a higher level of public agreement about the policy and a better understanding of its aims.

Analyses of the Different Rationales for Affirmative Action: Instrumental and Moral Justifications

As I note above, common justifications for affirmative action in higher education admissions typically fall into four substantive categories: *remediation*, highlighting that affirmative action compensates for past discrimination (Feinberg 1998); *economics*, highlighting affirmative action as one way to help disadvantaged people contribute to economic efficiency (Bowen and Bok 1998); *diversity*, highlighting affirmative action's role in increasing diversity on campus and the educational benefits that flow from it, as well as among officeholders in society (Chang 2001; Moses and Chang 2006); and *social justice*, highlighting affirmative action as one important tool in the quest for greater racial integration, equity, and justice (Anderson 2002, 2010; Moses 2001). These categories fall under two types of justification, instrumental and moral. Instrumental justifications view affirmative action policies merely as a means to an end; the policy serves the purpose of meeting a certain goal such as providing society with more workers from disadvantaged groups or making institutions of higher education more diverse places. Moral justifications appeal to deeper beliefs about what is right and good and how people ought to be treated; these can be backward looking or forward looking (Anderson 2002; Gutmann 1999; Jacobs 2004). The economics and diversity rationales fall most clearly under the instrumental type, and the remediation and social justice rationales fall under the moral type.

REMEDIATION The remedial rationale is a moral justification aimed at righting past wrongs and emphasizing compensatory, corrective action to rectify unfair treatment by race, ethnicity, and sex. Remediation was once the most prominent rationale used in the United States, until the courts showed it to be a viable rationale only in some specific cases of provable past discrimination, and the US Supreme Court found it to be a far less compelling rationale than arguments based on diversity (Marin and Horn 2008).

ECONOMICS A strongly instrumental rationale, the economic argument for affirmative action centers first on societies' need for more disadvantaged people to be educated and to join the workforce and contribute to the economy.[10] Economic efficiency justifies the need to develop more role models for disadvantaged youth so they will not be as disaffected and will instead learn the importance and possibility of becoming contributing members of society. In this case, "contributing" signifies making economic contributions and not using welfare services. The arguments related to economics have some force, particularly the notion that affirmative action contributes to role models for disadvantaged young people. Indeed, the research has paid some attention to the importance of role models for underrepresented students (e.g., Bowen and Bok 1998; Gándara 1995). However, appeal to affirmative action's role in increasing people's later economic productivity or engagement in mainstream economic affairs has not been as compelling as the diversity rationale, either in the public discourse or in the legal arena (*Grutter* 2003; Orfield, Marin, and Horn 2005). The *Grutter* court cited the importance of providing university access to people who can then return to their communities as a strong justification for allowing universities to consider race/ethnicity as one qualifying factor for admission. In that same case, the court primarily invoked the diversity rationale in its opinion (Moses and Chang 2006).

DIVERSITY Myriad researchers have found significant educational benefits of having diverse classrooms and campuses, specifically that they improve research quality, learning experiences, problem solving abilities, critical thinking skills, and preparation for life in a diverse society (e.g., Anderson 1995; Antonio et al. 2004; Chang 1999, 2001; Chang et al. 2003; Gurin 1999; Gurin, Dey, Hurtado, and Gurin 2002). The United States in particular has used this instrumental justification as part of a successful legal strategy for defending the use of race and ethnicity as valid qualifications in the university admissions process. This rationale is now, in fact, the dominant one invoked in the United States (Moses and Chang 2006). Stemming from Justice Lewis Powell's opinion in the *Bakke* decision, affirmative action is a compelling state interest because of educational benefits that flow from a diverse student body. Justice Powell explained that a diverse student body increases and deepens the opinions and perspectives present in classrooms and on campus, allowing for a richer learning environment (Orfield 2001; Shoemaker 2002). The diversity rationale became even more prominent after the 2003 *Grutter* decision. The University of Michigan defense in that case relied most heavily on the *Bakke* precedent to justify affirmative action in undergraduate and law school admissions (Elgass 2000; Marin and Horn 2008).

SOCIAL JUSTICE   The social justice[11] rationale focuses on racial integration, elimination of institutionalized inequalities, and equity in democratic participation (Anderson 2002; 2010; Gutmann 1999; Jacobs 2004; Young 1990). As Elizabeth Anderson (2010) argues, racial integration is important in providing opportunities to racial minorities and for fostering a democratic civil society. The social justice argument explains, on a profound level, why a society ought to act affirmatively to admit underrepresented students to higher education in greater numbers. In other words, we ought to support and argue for affirmative action policy because it is the right thing to do. Although some scholars mention the social justice rationale as important (Bell 2003; Fiss 1997; Moses 2002), the diversity rationale is most prominent (Fullinwider 1997; Moses and Chang 2006).

The United States' reluctance to embrace fully the social justice rationale for affirmative action has stemmed from a general shift away from the ideals of the civil rights movement (Graham 1990). The turn toward more instrumental rationales was partly strategic, with the intention of preserving the policy within a larger sociopolitical context marked by moral disagreement. Although egalitarians do not want the remedial or social justice rationales for affirmative action to be forsaken entirely, perhaps they have come to understand that libertarians likely would find the economics and diversity rationales somewhat more palatable, given their priority and emphasis on liberty. Libertarians could be swayed by a justification of affirmative action that appeals to its role in increasing educational and social opportunities. Such a justification would need to highlight how opportunities are increased by enhancing affirmative action beneficiaries' freedom through expanding their social context of choice, the context within which they make decisions about the future, participate in democratic politics, and contribute to the economic system (Anderson 2010; Moses 2001). Anderson (2002) explains it well:

> Unless disadvantaged racial groups are integrated into mainstream social institutions, they will continue to suffer from segregation and discrimination.

But the loss is not only theirs. It is a loss suffered by the American public at large in its failure fully to realize civil society—extensive social spaces in which citizens from all origins exchange ideas and cooperate on terms of equality—which is the indispensable social condition of democracy itself. (1270–71)

In addition, the concept of diversity has proven to have broad appeal (Moses and Chang 2006; Nussbaum 1997); as noted above, even a staunch affirmative action opponent like former president George W. Bush (2003), whose views stem from libertarian ideas, championed the importance of diversity.

These different facets of the prominent rationales demonstrate the complexities related to which justifications might appeal to egalitarians and which justifications might appeal to libertarians. The remedial rationale may have similar appeal to libertarians and egalitarians. Libertarians may agree on a moral level that when a person's liberty has been violated (as past discrimination certainly did), that compensation or remediation is appropriate. But they may get stuck on the difficulties of determining how to place blame on particular people or institutions for acts committed against particular people. Their problem with affirmative action as a remedial solution is a moral one in that it fails to identify accurately who should pay for past bad acts and who should receive the compensation for past harms. Egalitarians see the systemic nature of the discrimination and its societal effects and tend to see many in the majority as having benefited from past discrimination and many in disadvantaged groups having suffered from discrimination and its effects, therefore justifying the use of race-conscious policies like affirmative action. In addition, the social justice rationale for affirmative action is defined from an egalitarian perspective, but libertarians would argue that their claims against affirmative action are equally grounded in their social justice concerns. That is, their concern is that when the state intervenes through policies such as affirmative action, people act on the wrong moral incentives. They no longer view themselves as autonomous but instead as dependent on the state (or oppressed by the state). Their color-blindness argument is based on the moral idea that race should be irrelevant and therefore equality demands that it not be considered lest society continue to be fixated on race.

Given that different justificatory emphases for certain policies will appeal to those with different moral values and priorities, I think it important to have flexibility of justification for controversial policies like affirmative action. It is not necessary, either legally or sociopolitically, to limit the rationales for affirmative action available to stakeholders, scholars, or the courts.

There are different, and good, reasons for invoking the prominent rationales. Although I may personally prefer invoking the social justice rationale (see Moses 2010), any sort of mutual respect between those with conflicting values and perspectives, as well as moral-political compromise, likely will require flexibility in recognition of both strategic and moral-political justifications.

Conclusion

Egalitarians and libertarians share significant ideals and common justificatory frameworks that are relevant to affirmative action policy, yet the moral disagreement remains strong. Returning to the ideas about race and fairness from Justice Blackmun and Chief Justice Roberts, what can we make of this seeming paradox?

As we have seen herein, the debates surrounding affirmative action policy in higher education admissions have both a moral and political tenor. The enduring disagreement over affirmative action underscores the importance of examining moral disagreements over policy issues that have significant ramifications for how students are treated by the educational system and what educational opportunities they can enjoy. As Loury (2002) notes in the quotation that opens this chapter, we may not be able to rely on more research or evidence to spur people to compromise on this issue. Indeed, if reasonable people disagree so profoundly, we have to change the way we approach dialogue about the disagreements, focusing on what each can learn from the other and all can learn from the conflict (Sturgeon 1994). In this way, moral tragedies stemming from simplistic, narrowly self-interested, ideological, or poorly informed public policy decisions will be less likely to occur.

Approaching public dialogue and deliberation with aims conceived more broadly than decision making or consensus would allow for the kind of conversation that fosters deeper moral understanding between diverse citizens, in the service of justice. The idea is for dialogue to contribute to people's ability to stand in others' shoes, that is, take an empathetic perspective with regards to others' different beliefs and values. I agree with Green (1998) when he maintains that "life is fuller for all of us when we live it among *different* people, all respecting and identifying with each other in that difference" (199). A primary goal of dialogue and deliberation across difference is developing that fuller life, "of cooperation with others of different experiences in seeking common goals, [which] is also the only kind of life that will create the institutions of equal opportunity" (Green 1998,

199). It is not merely that I would like people to engage in dialogue so that they can learn to tolerate their sociopolitical differences, but rather that I would like to see people in dialogue together gaining a mutual respect for other reasonable[12] albeit different perspectives. This mutual respect will contribute to transcending "agreeing to disagree" relativism; indeed this is how we can move toward nonoppressive education policies through greater understanding of the different perspectives that surround a given policy issue.

In the next chapter I aim to provide more information on the affirmative action policy case in the larger sociopolitical context. I examine how political and legal discussions illustrate the moral disagreement about affirmative action. The next chapter focuses on how state ballot initiative campaigns use direct democratic processes to pursue legislative solutions to the deep moral disagreement about affirmative action. And as with Supreme Court decisions, although a number of proposed anti-affirmative action initiatives have passed, eliminating affirmative action in those states, again we see that the disagreement over race consciousness and equality has not dissipated. On the contrary, the anti-affirmative action ballot initiative campaigns fuel the conflicts over democratic ideals, as evidenced by voter (mis)understandings of the initiative language and intent, specifically the central concepts invoked within the initiative itself and within the campaigns surrounding the initiative.

FOUR

Ballot Initiatives, Moral Disagreement, and Ideas of Equality

This chapter examines the state ballot initiative, a legislative avenue for influencing affirmative action and other controversial education policies, one that uses direct democratic means to force statutory or state constitutional changes. Perhaps even more than court cases, ballot initiatives have brought the moral disagreement about affirmative action to the surface and into public discussion. The court cases have demonstrated somewhat the moral disagreements about affirmative action, especially, for example, in the Supreme Court justices' opinions and justifications for their decisions. Amicus briefs have also illustrated the differences and similarities of values and priorities held by opposing sides. Since 1978 the US Supreme Court has allowed the *Bakke* precedent to stand, albeit in a more restricted form. Nevertheless, libertarian opponents of affirmative action who adhere to color blindness in law and policy steadily have been using state ballot initiatives to further their own beliefs and ideas about affirmative action. The campaigns for and against these ballot initiatives highlight the differences between egalitarians and libertarians in a stark way. Indeed, the use of this kind of direct democratic legislative mechanism underscores how egalitarians and libertarians think about the democratic process and issues of equality. Conflicting values and conceptual interpretations are evident not only within the substantive policy issues under discussion, but also related to the method of legislative change itself. In a relevant recent development related to the use of state ballot initiatives to eliminate affirmative action policies, during the 2013–14 session the Supreme Court heard *Schuette v. Coalition to Defend Affirmative Action*, a case with broader implications for racial equality than one focused singularly on the constitutionality of affirmative action itself, as *Fisher* was. *Schuette* took up the question of the constitutionality of Michigan's Proposal 2, a ballot initiative that amended Michigan's state constitution to eliminate the consideration of race in public higher educa-tion admissions decisions, which passed in 2006 (Garces 2013b). The Sixth Circuit Court ruled that Proposal 2 is unconstitutional because it violates the equal protection clause of the Fourteenth Amendment. With what the *New York Times* Editorial Board (2014) called "a blinkered view on race in America," the US Supreme Court ruled against the Coalition to Defend Af-firmative Action on April 22, 2014. The justices ruled 6–2 (with Justice Elena Kagan recusing herself) that Michigan voters were permitted to eliminate affirmative action policies in public education, hiring, and contracting. Dis-senting Justices Sotomayor and Ruth Bader Ginsburg disagreed, saying that altering the political process through such a ballot initiative puts an undue burden on minority populations and violates the equal protection clause.

Because the direct democratic process provides an opportunity for public engagement, dialogue, and deliberation in a way that the legal disputes in court do not, in this chapter I focus on disputes about the ballot initiative process itself, as well as on how the moral disagreement about affirmative action plays out in this public political arena. In what follows, I describe and evaluate the ballot initiative process in general, with a particular focus on anti-affirmative action initiatives. I delve into the larger policy context, explaining how direct democracy functions in the United States. I move then to a discussion of the pros and cons of using the ballot initiative process, in which I pay special attention to how egalitarians and libertarians view those pros and cons. I begin by setting the background context for ballot initiative processes.

Ballot Initiatives as a Direct Democratic Avenue for Legislation

In the United States, twenty-four states currently permit state ballot initia-tives. Starting in the early 1900s, these initiatives were seen as powerful tools to challenge the undue influence of money in political processes. As Mark Smith (2002) makes clear,

> The original advocates of initiatives and referenda during the progressive era claimed that ballot measures could stimulate the public's political knowledge. If people gained a real voice in legislation by voting directly on issues . . . they would develop greater interest in and knowledge of politics that would carry beyond the specific measures voted on. (892)

Nevertheless, the use of ballot initiatives did not increase dramatically until the late 1970s. For example, in California between 1954 and 1974 there were 29 state ballot initiatives. From 1976 to 1996 there were 106 (HoSang 2010). Spending on initiative campaigns has also grown significantly (Gerber 1999; Smith and Tolbert 2004). State ballots often involve amendments to state constitutions, which involve complicated processes to undo once they pass.

Direct democracy is of three types: initiative, referendum, and recall. Depending on state rules, citizens need to gather a certain number of signatures to put an issue to popular vote. Herein I am concerned primarily with initiatives, also known as ballot measures. Initiatives involve placing a statutory measure or constitutional amendment on the ballot (Smith and Tolbert 2004). Such measures have covered myriad issues. Related to education, they have proposed, for example, to ban affirmative action in public higher education, mandate a teacher pay-for-performance system, and eliminate bilingual education (Ash 2008).

Some supporters of direct democracy claim that initiative processes overwhelmingly support what the majority of citizens want (rather than special interest groups). Invoking the priority of the ideal of liberty, libertarians in particular view the ballot initiative as a fair way to make law. Egalitarians seem to take a more measured approach to ballot initiatives, using them in some cases, but raising concerns when they seem to violate the ideals of equality or diversity. John Matsusaka (2004) characterized the debate over ballot initiatives as a struggle between those concerned about issues such as the power of money in initiative processes and those arguing that initiatives serve to foster freedom within democracy. Gutmann's idea of deliberative democracy is premised from the notion that democratic political life necessarily includes moral conflicts (Gutmann 1987; Gutmann and Thompson 1996). Ballot initiatives introduce challenges to democracy, as nonexpert citizens are asked to make decisions about education policies that directly affect their fellow citizens, like in the case of affirmative action.

Education policies placed on state ballots often impact minority populations directly (Farley 2014; Moses 2010; Sabato, Ernst, and Larson 2001). Yet they are decided by a process based on majority rule. Whereas in the past these policies often were determined by "experts"—policymakers and political representatives—citizens now often hold the power and responsibility, which some libertarians would argue is good for democracy (Gerber 1999; Smith and Tolbert 2004). In 2010 alone, 160 state-level initiatives were on the ballot in the United States. They concerned issues such as affirmative action, climate change, health care, and taxes (Prah 2010). Despite their apparent popularity as an avenue for legislation, their use is a contested matter in general, and particularly when they involve minority concerns.

Arguments for and against Direct Democratic Ballot Initiatives

There are three key arguments for direct democratic ballot initiatives: (1) they provide citizens access to the democratic process; (2) they function as a check on legislators and policymakers; and (3) they stimulate voter education and participation. The first two arguments come from the aggregative conception of democracy. It is not surprising that libertarians often support the use of ballot initiatives to make law. There are, in turn, three primary arguments against ballot initiatives: (1) moneyed interests play a disproportionate role, serving to corrupt campaigns; (2) most citizens are not informed enough for making certain decisions; and (3) the majoritarian intuition inherent in direct democracy too often tramples minority concerns (Broder 2000; Matsusaka 2004; Sabato, Ernst, and Larson 2001). These arguments come from the deliberative conception of democracy. In the sections following, I examine each of these pro and con arguments.

Arguments for the Use of Ballot Initiatives

Access

A strong argument in favor of direct democratic ballots is that they provide citizens access to the lawmaking process (Guetzloe 2001). According to libertarian advocates, each citizen has an equal opportunity to propose an initiative. Although some initiatives might restrict citizens' liberty, many believe that the majority vote as open access is a good in itself, regardless of the outcomes of that increased access (Gerber 1996). For egalitarians, the use of initiatives seems more complicated. Consider Oregon's 1990 seat belt law, which could be viewed as restricting citizens' liberty while also promoting the latest science on car safety. It required "all Oregonians to buckle up. . . . The bill was simple, people could use their own everyday experiences to make an informed decision, the money expended to qualify and pass the measure was modest, . . . and the policy change did not produce a host of unintended consequences" (Ellis 2002, 2). Similarly, in education policy, some citizen-initiated measures are amenable to both egalitarians and libertarians, in particular when related to local school bond issues.

A Check on Legislators

Perhaps the most broadly compelling argument for citizen-initiated ballots is that they provide the public with the opportunity to keep legislators in check. A common misunderstanding exists, however, about how citizens can indeed check legislative power. Earlier I mentioned that there are three common ballot measures: initiative, referendum, and recall. This is where referendum and recall come into play. The popular referendum serves well the purpose of checking on the legislature—through it, citizens can gather signatures to call for a vote on state legislation (Ellis 2002; Gerber 1996). The recall works in much the same way to call for a vote on a sitting elected official. With these avenues in place, there may be no need for the ballot initiative to serve as an additional check.

The body of research on ballot initiatives serving to check legislators does not reach clear conclusions. Whereas Elisabeth Gerber (1996) finds that direct democratic initiatives serve to make legislators more responsive to the public, Edward Lascher, Michael Hagen, and Steven Rochlin (1996) find just the opposite: "in none of these policy areas, however, does the presence of the initiative process significantly enhance the connection between public opinion and policy outcomes" (769). In examining the claim that the ballot initiative process makes government more responsive to public demands than would be the case under a purely representative system, their research contradicted "the claim that the presence of a direct ballot initiative process is associated with more responsive policies. Absent the initiative process, public opinion exerts a substantial and significant influence on state policies. . . . [I]n none of these policy areas, however, does the presence of the initiative process significantly enhance the connection between public opinion and policy outcomes" (769). Furthermore, the relationship between majority public opinion and policy outcomes is complex; it is not clear that policies should always reflect public opinion, especially as related to minority and social justice concerns.

Participation

Daniel Smith and Caroline Tolbert (2004) argue that although they understand the potential danger of direct democracy by ballot initiative, initiative processes could be very positive for democratic practices, as members of the public are provided with more education on the issues and voter turnout is higher when such initiatives are on the ballot. Similarly, Tolbert, John Grummel, and Smith (2001) find that ballot initiatives increase voter turnout, although only in presidential election years in states with a high number of issues on the ballot. In addition, Shaun Bowler and Todd Donovan (2000) find that voters are more capable than political scientists often give them credit for, that is, they are more capable to become informed about the issues up for vote and cast a thoughtful vote. One argument Bowler and Donovan make is that initiative campaigns actually promote voter engagement; they also argue that voters use the state ballot guides and that such a simple resource usually provides what voters need to come to an informed decision. Similarly, Donovan, Bowler, and David McCuan's (2001) research shows that voters get their information from official ballot summaries and media coverage of the ballot initiatives rather than campaign advertisements and messages. Of course, such confidence in official ballot summaries and the media may be misplaced; ballot summaries are notoriously confusing and misleading (Sabato, Ernst, and Larson 2001), and the media rarely provide the public with substantive information about ballot issues (Moses and Saenz 2008; Paguyo and Moses 2011). Another important question egalitarians would ask has to do with whether voters of color or low-income voters benefit from increased opportunities for participation (Gamble 1997).

Arguments against the Use of Ballot Initiatives

Power and Corruption

Several studies of ballot initiatives conclude that the effect of initiative campaigns on the democratic process frequently can be dangerous, with one important reason being that they are easily corrupted by the influence of money and power (Broder 2000; Ellis 2002; Sabato, Ernst, and Larson 2001; Stratman 2005). The concern from the left is that an individual or special interest group can use personal wealth or influence to push an issue before voters. Supporters of ballot initiatives argue that citizens should be free to propose initiatives despite such concerns. In addition, the money and power of interest groups or individual sponsors may have less impact than some believe: "Wealthy economic interest groups are severely constrained by the institutional and behavioral hurdles inherent in the direct legislation process. They cannot and do not use their financial resources to 'buy' legislation that is detrimental to broader citizen interests" (Gerber 1999, 20). Yet, as egalitarians worry, in numerous cases wealthy individuals or groups spearhead initiative campaigns. For instance, this was evident when a perennial ballot initiative figure, Bill Sizemore, a former candidate for governor in Oregon, registered a proposed ballot initiative to put a two-year cap on the amount of time English-language learners (ELLs) can receive bilingual instruction. Sizemore opposes bilingual education, endorsing instead an English immersion approach. Both educators and immigrant rights groups disagree with the immersion approach, arguing that it limits educational opportunities and that ELLs should be provided with native language instruction and English as a second language classes for as long as necessary before being mainstreamed into all-English classrooms. This is an example of a wealthy and powerful individual putting a pet issue up for popular vote, using the political system to further his own moral and political values and ideals.

Similarly, the campaigns and wording of the initiatives themselves can be deceptive and misleading (Farley, Gaertner, and Moses 2013; Moses et al. 2010). Whether intentional or unintentional, the net result is that voters may think they are voting for one thing when in fact voting for something quite different. Even America's founders anticipated the problem of deception in direct democracy. As James Madison (1788) wrote,

> there are particular moments in public affairs, when the people stimulated by some irregular passion, or some illicit advantage, or misled by the artful misrepresentations of interested men, may call for measures which they themselves will afterwards be the most ready to lament. (¶ 7)

Two education policy examples illustrate this: in 2000, when Arizona was voting on an anti-bilingual education initiative, the title was "English for the Children." This title implied incorrectly that supporters of bilingual education were not already concerned about teaching nonnative speakers English. In addition, all of the anti-affirmative action ballot initiatives have been entitled "Civil Rights Initiatives," although they actually aim to abolish a traditional civil rights policy. In Colorado, the chief spokesperson for the proposed anti-affirmative action initiative, libertarian Jessica Peck Corry, claimed that it would not eliminate affirmative action. When questioned further, she explained that it would simply require that all affirmative action and equal opportunity programs include white people and men (Corry 2008). Richard Ellis (2002) points out that the way initiatives are worded and framed makes a huge difference in whether people support them. For example, people react more negatively to "preferential treatment" than to "affirmative action" (77). The wording of the anti-affirmative action proposals passed in all states, but Oklahoma omitted the phrase "affirmative action." When a Houston city ballot initiative proposed to end "affirmative action" in public employment and contracting, the measure was defeated. In Colorado, research on the factors that affected the vote on Amendment 46 found that even though the initiative failed by a slim margin, if the ballot language had been clear, it likely would have failed by a much larger margin (Moses et al. 2010).

Information

In his critique of the US democratic system, Jim Holt (2006) points out, "most citizens have no economic incentive to learn enough about what politicians do to vote intelligently. Nearly half of American voters acquiesce in their infantilization by not voting at all" (18). I would not go as far as Holt, but it may indeed be problematic to leave some important questions related to educational opportunities in the hands of voters who may not be meaningfully informed on relevant policy issues and consequences. David Magleby (1989) points out that initiative campaigns have a strong impact on swaying voters who are less informed about the options. He concludes that powerful policy players can and do use initiative campaigns to control information about the ballot initiatives and their consequences.

Downplaying this concern, proponents of direct democracy would point out that there is no guarantee that experts or legislators would make better, more equitable education policy than voters, citing, for example, the oft-criticized No Child Left Behind Act. But a crucial idea behind representative democracy is that legislators are accountable to the people. By contrast voters are not in practice accountable to anyone. Nevertheless, Gerber (1996) argues that the threat of ballot initiatives prompt state legislators to listen more to their constituents. She finds that in states where ballot initiatives are used, legislators actually are more likely to pass legislation that mirrors the preferences of the general population. However, as Gerber herself points out, her model was filled with assumptions that would probably never mirror any real-world situation of policymaking. For instance, she assumed that all actors in the process have complete information and are able to act rationally, an assumption often held by libertarian theorists.

Even the most informed voters rely on the media for much of their ballot and political information (Chaffee and Frank 1996; Druckman 1995; Graber 1994; Project for Excellence in Journalism 2004; Roberts and Klibanoff 2006). Recent research on print media coverage of the anti-affirmative action initiatives on Michigan's and Colorado's ballots found that coverage most often does not provide meaningful or substantive information on ballot initiatives (Moses and Saenz 2008; Paguyo and Moses 2011). This is one reason that Ellis (2002) maintains that "when a policy has complex and far-reaching consequences for government and society, the initiative process is a particularly poor lawmaking instrument" (3). I should point out that I am not trying to make the argument that US citizens cannot be trusted with important democratic responsibilities, only that egalitarians question direct democracy as a way for citizens to exercise those responsibilities regarding issues of race-conscious education policy.[1]

Minority Concerns

The framers of the US Constitution had important reasons to advocate for an overall system of representative rather than direct democracy. For example, they believed that there would be problems with majorities trumping minorities regarding controversial issues (Epstein 1984; Sabato, Ernst, and Larson 2001). In 1829 at Virginia's Constitutional Convention, Madison warned: "in Republics, the great danger is, that the majority may not sufficiently respect the rights of the minority" (Madison 1829, ¶ 1). Race egalitarians worry nearly two centuries later that Madison's concern is substantiated by the ballot initiatives discussed herein, those affecting the educational opportunities of people of color.

According to Matsusaka (2004), the primary point of disagreement about initiatives is the question of whose interests are served most often. Indeed, a breakdown of the vote on Michigan's Proposal 2, for example, shows that minority concerns were neglected. This point—what Lani Guinier (1994) calls the "tyranny of the majority" (20)—is perhaps the most crucial reason egalitarians are skeptical about the education-policy-by-ballot-initiative phenomenon (Moses 2010). I agree with Guinier's point that "in a racially divided society, majority rule may be perceived as majority tyranny" (3), and indeed would take a step further to say that majority rule might not only be *perceived* as majority tyranny, it might *be* such tyranny.

Education policy often is concerned with the most profound issues of opportunity and justice. Although, as libertarians maintain, citizens are capable of fair thinking and should be free to participate in direct democracy in any way they choose, the problems sketched above are substantive. In any education policy ballot, the one common crucial element is public dialogue and deliberation: "public dialogue is critical to represent all perspectives; no one viewpoint should be permitted to monopolize, distort, caricature, or shape public debate. The tyranny of The Majority is just as much a problem of silencing minority viewpoints as it is of excluding minority representatives or preferences" (Guinier 1994, 19–20).

The Tyranny of the Majority and Ballot Initiative Reforms

To be sure, some initiatives may be useful tools of direct democracy. But to mitigate the potential negative effects on equality of educational opportunity resulting from ballot initiatives, significant reform is needed (Goodin 2003). Although ballot initiative supporters argue that detrimental effects on minorities are drastically overstated (Hajnal, Gerber, and Louch 2002), research shows otherwise. Examining ballots related to civil rights proposed from 1959 to 1993, Barbara Gamble (1997) found that of the 74 such initiatives, 78 percent constituted a defeat for minority interests, while only a third of all other initiatives were approved. When it comes to education policy, ballot initiative reform is crucial, given threats to the ideals of equality and diversity.

Supporters of reform have advocated wholesale changes, such as requiring all ballot initiatives to succeed only by supermajority (Ellis 2002). They have also advocated more moderate reforms: increased voter information; greater transparency of campaign finance, so voters could assess the motives of an initiative's funders; public subsidies available to ballot campaigns to mitigate the role of money; detailed voter guides with pro and con information, and independent analyses of the initiative's likely consequences (Farley 2014; Sabato, Ernst, and Larson 2001).

While I agree with some of these suggestions, I want to add one broader point stemming from democratic theory: reform of the ballot initiative process should focus on eliminating—or at least mitigating—significant flaws. One way to do this in a democratic manner is to follow Gutmann's (1999) limits on political authority. The principle of nonrepression in particular limits the state's ability to use education "to restrict rational deliberation of competing conceptions of the good life" (44). Ballot initiatives proposing to end policies that foster equal opportunity for underrepresented minorities too often violate the principle of nonrepression by serving to restrict the self-determination and social contexts of choice of students of color (Moses 2002). Since the 1996 passage of Proposition 209, the numbers of students of color in the UC system have not kept pace with increasing shares of students of color in the state and have decreased at the two most selective campuses (Moses, Yun, and Marin 2009; Saenz 2010). Overall in states where affirmative action has been banned via ballot initiative, the enrollment of underrepresented students of color has decreased at top-tier colleges and universities (Backes 2012; Hinrichs 2012). Egalitarians hold that such consequences of anti-affirmative action ballot initiatives demonstrate that the ballot initiative process harms higher education's ability to meet its equality and diversity goals. This in turn results in limits on self-determination and social contexts of choice for individual students. Libertarians, on the other hand, may see the outcomes of these ballot initiatives as just because all applicants are being treated the same.

For egalitarians, the constraints for underrepresented students of color reveal majority tyranny in action. According to Gutmann (1999), "if democracies are to govern themselves, they must remain free to make mistakes in educating their children, as long as those mistakes do not discriminate against some children or prevent others from governing themselves freely in the future. The promise of the principles of nonrepression and nondiscrimination is just this: to support a strong democracy without sanctioning majority tyranny or sacrificing self-government in the future" (97–98). The negative consequences of anti-affirmative action ballots violate Gutmann's key principle of nonrepression. Consequently, direct democratic education policymaking may serve to neglect minority rights, resulting in the *legally sanctioned* denial of equality of educational opportunity to underrepresented students of color.

Conclusion

Because eliminating race-conscious education policies often negatively affects equality and diversity (Contreras 2005; Moses, Yun, and Marin 2009; Saenz 2008), it is important to consider whether the simple majoritarian rule exemplified by ballot initiatives serves the basic ideal of equality agreed on by both egalitarian and libertarian theorists. This can be understood as part of a dispute between aggregative democratic theorists (including proceduralists) and deliberative democratic theorists (including epistemic and substantive theorists) (Goodin 2003; Gutmann and Thompson 2004; Young 2000). Aggregative conceptions of democracy consider citizens' preferences to be given, that is, preferences are taken at face value and justifications are viewed as irrelevant to fair democratic processes. From the analysis in chapter 3, we can see how aggregative theorists' ideas parallel those of libertarian political theory. By contrast, deliberative conceptions consider citizens' reasons (i.e., justifications) for their sociopolitical preferences to be central to the democratic process (Gutmann and Thompson 2004; Young 2000). Regarding the important question of "how to make legitimate decisions for the society as a whole in the face of fundamental disagreement" (Gutmann and Thompson 2004, 14), aggregative theories typically turn to majoritarian methods of governance (i.e., let voters or elected representatives decide). Egalitarian theorists who focus on the importance of deliberative democracy, Gutmann and Thompson (2004) argue that the aggregative conception is flawed because it "fundamentally accepts and may even reinforce existing distributions of power in society" (16). Yet a difficulty with deliberative conceptions is that there is no clear way to resolve disagreements and make public policy decisions, so the default often has been to rely on a procedure like voting, which is not necessarily a deliberative process. In addition, within deliberative democratic theory, there is disagreement over deliberation's instrumental value (i.e., "as a means of arriving at good policies") and its expressive value (i.e., "as a manifestation of mutual respect among citizens") (21). Deliberative theorists maintain that the fair procedures libertarians privilege and the substantive principles egalitarians privilege both need to be part of the democratic process. What I am arguing for herein is that education policy disputes that resist easy resolutions ought to be considered and examined in dialogue with others. At the very least such dialogues can foster mutual respect among citizens. And there is potential for the dialogues to foster better policies as well. Chapter 5 focuses on these possible outcomes of dialogue in the context of deliberative democratic theory.

Gutmann and Thompson's (1996, 2004) deliberative democratic framework is characterized by discussions in which people publicly provide reasons for their views in a broadly accessible way. The shift from experts to citizens means that to promote fair decisions, voters need to have access to meaningful information. In light of the increasing role of the public, there is a need for researchers and scholars (i.e., experts) to contribute such information.

In the case of education, scholars have the responsibility of providing credible information that helps advance public deliberation (Wachbroit 1998). This is even more important because the public's role has been expanding through direct democratic initiatives. Public deliberation over critical issues can function to clarify contested values, increase public understanding, foster people's willingness to reconsider their views, and increase communication between opposing sides on a given issue. This is especially important for policies that appeal to values that can be divisive and misunderstood.

Making decisions about education policies about which there is moral disagreement is not easy. The policy's design, goals, outcomes, and moral implications must be negotiated. While scholars can expand the way their expertise is communicated and used, the larger question that arises from the education-policy-by-ballot-initiative phenomenon concerns how it affects key democratic ideals. Defining politics in terms of voting is not enough—we have to think in terms of democratic participation more broadly, so that, as Guinier (2008) explains, "citizens and their representatives work together to change the metric of success from winning elections to building the kind of collective intelligence and collective power that provides more robust sources of democratic accountability and legitimacy" (4). Without such efforts, ballot initiatives on equality-related education policies often will trample the interests of students of color, which is detrimental for equality, liberty, and diversity.

In the next chapter, I describe and examine a promising avenue through which scholars can engage with members of the public: community dialogues on controversial issues of education policy. Although the deep moral disagreements about such policies are difficult if not impossible to transcend fully, the disagreements provide opportunities for fruitful dialogue and deliberation leading to greater mutual understanding, and—potentially—policy compromises, all of which are important for democracy.

FIVE

Deliberative Democracy and Policy Dialogue

WITH LAUREN P. SAENZ AND AMY FARLEY LOBUE

Given the deep disagreement about race-conscious education policies in general and about affirmative action in particular, characterized by differing interpretations of the central concepts and ideals thrown around in the debates, it is difficult to know what to do about it. As the case of affirmative action and the concomitant political and legislative debates demonstrate, moral disagreements may appear to be—and sometimes are—intractable. Deliberative democratic theorists tout the merits of dialogue and deliberation as effective ways to bridge differences of values and opinion, ideally resulting in agreement, or perhaps more often resulting in greater mutual understanding. Proponents of learning through dialogue tout the merits of talk as transformative and expansive (Graves 2013; Mezirow 2000). For my part, I have come to believe in the potential of public dialogue to inform participants about different views, foster questions about one's own beliefs and perspectives, and reach more profound understandings about opposing or conflicting moral positions. This is all the more important given the political context of education policy ballot initiatives in numerous states, as noted especially in chapters 2 and 4. As such, I wanted to test my belief in dialogue in some way, to see whether indeed public dialogues could provide a way toward greater understanding, better informed politics, and living with moral disagreement in productive and democratic ways.

In this chapter I share my research on public community dialogues about affirmative action policy. Although admittedly a small study, combined with the empirical research literature on the promise of democratic dialogue and deliberation, it provides evidence of the illuminating power in informative and inclusive conversations, as we asked the following questions. Could dialogue mitigate disagreements about controversial race-conscious education policies? Could it foster greater understanding? My research team and

I set out to investigate these questions, especially as related to how dialogue participants understood and justified affirmative action.

Given the fraught current legal and legislative policy context for affirmative action policies, my research team and I saw the public debate over an anti-affirmative action ballot initiative in our state as an opportunity to use our expertise to help people in the community learn about and discuss education-related issues relevant to the upcoming vote. At the same time we wanted to study these efforts to see whether indeed they would make a difference in people's policy knowledge and understanding. With education policy ballot initiatives becoming increasingly prevalent, voters across the country are given the opportunity to decide education policy through a direct democratic process. In 2008, Coloradans voted on Amendment 46, which was intended to end affirmative action in the state. In a reversal of past trends and despite numerous polling predictions to the contrary, Colorado voters defeated the ballot initiative, by fewer than 40,000 votes. As I mention in the previous chapter, although researchers argue whether the increasing role of the public in policy decisions is a good thing for democracy (Bowler and Donovan 2000; Gerber 1999; Moses and Farley 2011; Moses and Saenz 2008; Smith and Tolbert 2004), there is a role for researchers (i.e., experts) in fostering and providing public information.

As such, our study was conceived with two purposes: (1) to investigate how scholar-facilitated community dialogues on affirmative action affected dialogue participants' affirmative action knowledge, beliefs, and voting behavior; and (2) to bring researcher expertise to bear on affirmative action policy, as Coloradans prepared to vote on an anti-affirmative action ballot initiative. In this chapter, we describe the design, implementation, and findings of this study, in an effort to share a promising opportunity for community dialogue. Our findings include analyses of data from dialogue participant questionnaires, the dialogues, and follow-up interviews. Through the questionnaires, participants responded to questions regarding their knowledge and beliefs about, and position for or against, affirmative action. (See appendices A, B, and C for the pre-, post-, and post-post-questionnaires and appendix D for the follow-up interview questions.) From the questionnaires and interview data sources, we wanted to learn how participation in community dialogues on affirmative action may affect participants' knowledge and beliefs about affirmative action, as well as how it may affect their political decision making about affirmative action policy.

We first expand on my earlier description of the theories that guided our data collection and analysis, and then situate this topic in the literature on the impact of deliberative dialogues like those conducted in this study.

Overall, we found that deliberative dialogues have the potential to educate participants on the substantive issues related to the moral disagreement about affirmative action. The community dialogue participants learned new information and grew in their understanding of affirmative action policy, although this growth differed by participants' race and age in particular. Generally, participants' attitudes toward affirmative action became more positive over the course of the dialogue. Further, many participants indicated that the dialogue experience influenced their personal decision about Amendment 46, and participants generally agreed that they were more likely to engage in deliberation on policy issues as a result of the dialogue experience. Participants had a positive deliberative experience, although their overall satisfaction was related to their pre-dialogue attitude toward affirmative action.

Expanded Consideration of Deliberative Democratic Theory

According to Gutmann and Thompson's (1996, 2004) theory of deliberative democracy, public deliberation on social policy issues is a necessary good. The design of our study and subsequent analyses relied on deliberative democratic theory. I mentioned some of the aims of and controversies surrounding deliberative democratic theory in earlier chapters. Here I want to take a moment to expand on those explanations, which focused more on my conceptual analyses, so as to provide a more nuanced sense of how this group of theories served to inform the empirical research.

Deliberative democratic theorists pose an alternative to aggregative or participatory democracy, arguing that citizens and society benefit from a deliberative process when they are confronted with moral disagreements (Gutmann and Thompson 1996, 2004). Democratic deliberation requires citizens to present their reasons and arguments in a public setting; individuals challenge one another and are challenged. In short, citizens come to understand and refine their own beliefs in the face of these challenges. In particular, Gutmann and Thompson (2004) argue for what they call the "principle of the economy of moral disagreement," whereby citizens ought to strive to provide justifications for their policy views and decisions that "minimize their differences with their opponents" (7). Through structured community dialogues, we aimed to put Gutmann and Thompson's theories into practice. Our philosophical interests led us to test both the feasibility and the implications of operationalizing deliberative democratic theory. That is, we attempted to create a setting built on deliberative democratic principles to explore a controversial moral issue, with the intent of describing and analyzing the implementation and impact of such an approach.

Typically, deliberative democratic theory is applied in the context of collective decision making, in situations in which groups are asked to find common ground and come to a mutually acceptable decision. Our dialogues did not require a decision by the group; they attempted to provide both information and a space within which people could present their reasons and arguments in a public setting, as part of a deliberative democracy. This way, participants would gain valuable information about affirmative action policy that they could then use to make their individual voting decision on Amendment 46. The Amendment 46 vote provided a unique context in which to study deliberative dialogues regarding a contentious, moral disagreement. The proliferation of the ballot initiative introduces new challenges to democracy, as, in the case of affirmative action, relatively nonexpert citizens are asked to decide individually on a race-conscious education policy that directly affects their fellow citizens. As such, voters are weighing in on the moral disagreement about affirmative action, and there is a direct policy consequence from ballot initiative votes.

Deliberative democratic theory traditionally has maintained what Mark Button and David Ryfe (2005) call a "normative thrust toward consensus and mutual agreement" (29). The design of our community dialogues altered the course of the "normative thrust" away from collective decision making and toward educative dialogue, reason giving, and public information. Participants were not asked to arrive at a compromised, mutual decision; rather, they were offered the opportunity to express their opinions and knowledge on a policy matter that affects the greater public. This was an intentional shift, designed not to move away from normative conceptions of deliberative democracy but to explore its educative effects in public settings. Thus, we focused not just on the potential outcomes of democratic deliberation, but also on its intrinsic value (which, in the end, may prove to be an outcome as well).

Deliberative democracy borrows from the traditions of John Stuart Mill, John Dewey, Jürgen Habermas, and John Rawls. It endeavors "to provide the most justifiable conception for dealing with moral disagreement in politics" (Gutmann and Thompson 2004, 10). To this end, deliberative democracy aims to legitimize collective decision making; encourage the public to provide public-centered perspectives; advance a respectful, mutual decision-making process; and to correct the mistakes of both citizens and officials. More generally, the claim of deliberative democratic theory is that a greater understanding of others' perspectives will lead to more productive dialogue about issues that are often sources of moral disagreement. Deliberative democracy, from Gutmann and Thompson's (2004) perspective, is the most promising way of holding citizens accountable to one another. And, we would add, it seems to be a promising approach to dialogue and mutual respect and understanding.

A deliberative perspective encourages greater public participation in and understanding of public policy debates by demanding that citizens abide by the principles of reciprocity, publicity, and accountability (Gutmann and Thompson 1996; Jacobs, Cook, and Delli Carpini 2009). Deliberative democratic theory places moral discussion in political life at center to cope with fundamental conflicts in values and ideology. In general, deliberative democracy is characterized by three conditions that regulate and structure the deliberative *process* of politics: (1) reciprocity, by which reason giving and justification for mutually binding policies are seen as a mutual endeavor; (2) publicity, which stipulates that policymakers, researchers, officials, and members of the public in general should have to justify their decisions and actions in public; and (3) accountability, which requires those who make policy decisions to answer to those who are bound by those policies (Gutmann and Thompson 1996, 2004). In addition to these three conditions, Gutmann and Thompson (1996) outline three substantive principles that serve to govern the *content* of policy deliberations: (1) basic liberty, which controls what government and society can demand of people and what people can demand of one another; (2) basic opportunity, which concerns the distribution of goods necessary for pursuing a good life (e.g., basic income); and (3) fair opportunity, which has to do with the distribution of socially valuable goods.

Critics of the deliberative democratic approach have pointed out that its emphasis on rational argument may neglect or devalue other modes of communication and participation. Although she is sympathetic to deliberative democratic theory, Young (1996) argues for a "communicative democracy" (120). This communicative democracy would not privilege rational argumentation in democratic deliberation; instead it would add greeting, rhetoric, and storytelling to argument as ways of communicating within democratic deliberations that are responsive to the need to "speak across difference" (129). As Young explains, greeting includes acknowledgment of others. Rhetoric includes the use of ways of speaking that appeal to people's emotions and feelings, such as figures of speech, images, and humor. And storytelling serves to link people using the empathy that often comes through narrative. Young (1996) suggests that to ensure the inclusion of diverse and nonmainstream viewpoints, such sociocultural practices need to be included in deliberation, both in theory and in practice. Gutmann and Thompson (2004) maintain that the communicative practices championed by Young fit into this framework as part of the way citizens give reasons and present arguments.

A deliberative democracy relies on the primary principle of *reciprocity* to foster policy discussions and debates that are respectful and inclusive and that encourage deeper understanding of the content of moral disagreements. The principle of reciprocity, in a sense, sets the ground rules for deliberation. Through the formal guidelines we put forward to shape the civil tenor of our community dialogues, we endeavored to apply these ideals to a real-world deliberative dialogue in the community. We operated from the assumption that an understanding of the content of moral disagreements is especially important in education policy. In principle, it is a good idea for citizens in a democracy to be well informed about the policies that are in place or being considered. But there are more pressing reasons. Making uninformed judgments without engaging with the content of moral disagreements is dangerous. As I have argued elsewhere (Moses 2004), this can lead to policy decisions that are simplistic, self-interested, or poorly informed, thus leading to potential "moral tragedies."[1] Young (2000), too, notes that a strong normative link exists between deliberative democracy and justice, in contrast to aggregative or representative democracy, which can lead to or perpetuate injustices.

Deliberative democracy supports expanding decision making to the public sphere in addition to the private sphere, by bringing together constituents and asking individuals to offer public reasons for their views. The ballot initiative process essentially narrows decision making to the private sphere. Voters most often deliberate and decide privately; hence their arguments are rarely exposed to public deliberation. Following deliberative democratic theory (Gutmann and Thompson 1996), our research was grounded in the idea that public deliberation is necessary when initiatives are put to a popular vote to foster a more informed voting public and greater mutual understanding across moral disagreements, with the goal of promoting effective, equitable education policy.

Deliberative democracy in practice is fertile ground for both philosophical and empirical research and can provide a model for future avenues of similar research. Up until the last decade or so, however, these fields have evolved separately (Barabas 2004). Recent empirical investigations have examined the feasibility of applied deliberative democracy, but tensions remain. Significant difficulties exist, for example, in implementing the normative principles of deliberative democracy in practical settings (Button and Mattson 1999; Walsh 2007). Yet there is a growing body of literature suggesting significant civic benefits to deliberative engagement.

The Impact of Deliberative Dialogues

Dialogues can take many different forms including citizen juries, deliberative polling, consensus conferences, and intergroup dialogues, to name some of the common types (Gastil and Levine 2005). *Citizens' juries* bring together a group of randomly chosen citizens to deliberate on a particular issue (Smith and Wales 2000). James Fishkin and Robert Luskin's (2005) *deliberative polling* exposes random samples of people to balanced information and encourages them to weigh opposing arguments in discussions with people holding different views and then collects their resulting opinions. *Consensus conferences* are described as citizen juries plus town hall meetings and have mainly been used to evaluate science and technology questions (Einsiedel and Eastlick 2000). *Intergroup dialogue* is a version of community dialogue that focuses on bringing together college students or community members from different social identity groups to discuss issues related to difference and social justice (Schoem et al. 2001; Walsh 2007; Zúñiga et al. 2007). Deliberative dialogues of all sorts allow participants the space and opportunity to engage collectively in these important social and political issues as part of democratic participation.

There are typically several characteristics that define community, small-group, and other types of dialogue. First, and common to all types of dialogue, are that they are largely face-to-face (Fishkin and Luskin 2005; Ryfe 2002; Schoem et al. 2001; Weeks 2000). Second, some dialogues are intended to be one-time events, while others are intended to be a series of dialogues sustained over a period of time. Third, the dialogue can be aimed at decision making or some kind of direct action, or it can be discussion oriented, without a particular immediate decision in mind (Fishkin and Luskin 2005; Pelletier et al. 1999; Ryfe 2002; Schoem et al. 2001; Weeks 2000).

The research on dialogues demonstrates that participants often leave dialogues with greater knowledge and understanding of the issues that were taken up (Andersen and Hansen 2007; Barabas 2004; Einsiedel and Eastlick 2000; Fishkin and Luskin 2005; McMillan and Harriger 2002; Smith and Wales 2000; Weeks 2000). We know from follow-up qualitative interviews with one-quarter of the dialogue participants in our study that the dialogue experience increased information about affirmative action and influenced participants' views on the issue. For example, a graduate student participant shared how the dialogue affected him: "I wasn't sure how I was going to vote on Amendment 46, and going through the process of the forum was very beneficial in shaping my opinion. We had a pretty diverse group and one of the things I got out of the forum was that it really is, well there are still problems with affirmative action and how it is implemented, but there is more of a benefit having it in place than not having it at all." In addition to individual effects, dialogue participants may go on to increase their civic participation and take civic action in their communities (Jacobs, Cook, and Delli Carpini 2009; Walsh 2007). In another study, Illinois dialogue participants later advocated for a more diverse police force and fire department, resulting in three new hires'from underrepresented groups (Walsh 2007). In the context of deliberative polling, dialogue participants gained information; their opinions changed, in both directions; and there was a positive relationship between gain in information and change in opinion (Fishkin and Luskin 2005). In addition, several studies of intergroup dialogue have shown that participants gain awareness of issues of difference, power, and justice; get to know and engage with people of different races and ethnicities; and take action for social justice (Gurin, Nagda, and Lopez 2004; Hurtado 2001; Nagda 2006; Nagda, Gurin, and Johnson 2005; Walsh 2007). While this research is useful in thinking about the results from dialogues generally, the deliberative dialogues used in our study were different in several key ways from the intergroup dialogues cited above, including the participant population and the length of time in deliberation. Whereas the deliberative community dialogues in our study were meant to be one-time experiences, the intergroup dialogues in many of the studies cited above were meant to be a series of dialogue sessions over time (Schoem et al. 2001). Both types, however, aim to be a democratic practice.

Taken as a whole, the results of the research literature considered here are complex. Consider that Jason Barabas (2004), in a study using propensity score matching to examine the effects of a deliberation about Social Security, found that deliberation indeed increased issue knowledge, but this was dependent on the quality of the comments and participants' ability to be open minded. Some studies have shown that participants can end up more anxious and frustrated or less open to other viewpoints (Ryfe 2005; Schkade, Sunstein, and Hastie 2006). In her research on intergroup community dialogues in multiple cities, Katherine Walsh (2007) found that participants in such dialogues may learn more about their differences than their similarities to others in the dialogue group. Others have found large-scale applications of deliberative practice feasible and effective (e.g., Weeks 2000). Ryfe (2005) noted also that people can walk away from the same deliberation with different senses of how it went, and that is because it involves an assessment of one's self in relation to others. In addition, political power, social status, and self-interest often are at play within dialogue sessions (Andersen and Hansen 2007; Davidson and Moses 2012; Mendelberg and Oleske 2000).

These issues seem likely to affect if and how participants learn from their deliberative experiences.

Our results both support and complement the findings of previous studies, as we discuss in the results section below. For example, Graham Smith and Corinne Wales's (2000) study of a citizen jury in the United Kingdom showed changes in preferences to be widespread, as well as strong effects on political understanding and participation. Our study also suggests that participants gained political issue knowledge. This finding underscores the idea that deliberative dialogues have significant promise of positive effects, whether the outcomes are related to increased understanding, democratic participation, or political decision making (Button and Ryfe 2005). Furthermore, we are also interested in the cumulative effects of deliberation; the data presented herein suggests that if individuals find deliberative opportunities worthwhile (i.e., they learn new information), they may seek out more such opportunities. Researchers have begun to document what can be considered the secondary effects of deliberative engagement: transforming public opinions and behaviors, changing public officials' opinions and behaviors, and impacting strategic political choices (see, e.g., Burkhalter, Gastil, and Kelshaw 2002; Chambers 2003; Delli Carpini, Cook, and Jacobs 2004; Gastil 2008). More research is needed on the long-term impacts of deliberation. Empirical investigations of deliberative democracy in practice can help to clarify the conditions for its successful implementation.

Data Sources and Methods

Conducting deliberative dialogues is not without precedent. In designing the dialogues for this project, we drew from several models, including the National Issues Forum (2011), the Public Conversations Project (2006; Herzig and Chasin 2006), and ChoiceDialogues (Fishkin and Rosell 2004). We included the common elements across all three: well-trained facilitators, small-group dialogue sessions, and specific, relevant, "expert" information to which all participants had access.

Toward this end, a group of nine education policy researchers (led by my coauthors on this chapter, Lauren Saenz and Amy Lobue, and me) organized and facilitated a dozen community dialogues throughout the Denver metropolitan area in the two months prior to the 2008 election. The dialogues addressed affirmative action policy more broadly rather than just Amendment 46. We undertook an ambitious exploratory, mixed-method multiple case study research design. Each dialogue represented a "case" that we studied as an individual unit as well as a part of the whole, to understand the larger phenomenon of the impact of deliberative democratic dialogue on political knowledge and decision making. Our data sources included the following: (1) community dialogue sessions, which were video and/or audio recorded (and fully transcribed for analysis); (2) pre- and post-questionnaires, which were administered to the seventy-nine participants immediately before and after the dialogue; and (3) follow-up interviews and post-dialogue questionnaires with a select group of participants (N=19).

Each dialogue began with introductions, both from facilitators and participants, to allow everyone to learn about the other people in the room and their motivations for attending the forum. They then watched two video clips from a debate about affirmative action sponsored by Intelligence Squared. One clip showed Tim Wise, an affirmative action supporter, and the other showed John McWhorter, an affirmative action opponent. Each shared popular arguments for and against affirmative action. After the video clips, facilitators asked participants the following open-ended question, to initiate the interactive portion of the dialogue: "What personal experiences of being treated fairly or unfairly influence your perspective on affirmative action?" Although we did provide the facilitators with a fact sheet on affirmative action that they could use to provide information if directly asked, facilitators were otherwise not active in the dialogue. In general, participants were asked to share their experiences; question and challenge themselves and each other; and grapple meaningfully with the content, philosophies, and potential effects of affirmative action. During the dialogue, participants responded in turn to a set of open-ended prompts and were allowed to "pass" on a question and then encouraged to return to it later if desired. Participants were also asked to agree to a set of ground rules to guide their conversations (i.e., listening respectfully, speaking for themselves and allowing others to do the same, not criticizing the views of others). As mentioned above, we did not ask participants to arrive at a shared decision. Rather, we were interested primarily in improving the quality of public dialogue on affirmative action by providing citizens with substantive information and offering them the space and tools with which to engage in democratic deliberation.

Prior to and immediately following each community dialogue, facilitators administered pre- and post-questionnaires to each of the seventy-nine participants across the twelve dialogues. The pre-post design allowed us to measure directly reported changes in attitudes and beliefs following dialogue participation. Additionally, we readministered the post-questionnaire and conducted follow-up interviews with nineteen volunteers to assess how any changes to beliefs and attitudes were maintained or changed several weeks following the dialogue; these follow-up questionnaires also allowed us to obtain information on how participants ultimately voted on Amendment 46 and whether they thought their dialogue experience affected their vote.

Questionnaire Data

Relying on the literature on affirmative action, members of the research team developed pre- and post-questionnaires to collect data in three primary areas: (a) participant substantive knowledge of both Colorado and national affirmative action policies, including current constitutional limitations; (b) participant attitudes toward affirmative action policy; and (c) participant reactions to and assessment of the deliberative dialogue experience (Moses 2002; Moses and Saenz 2008). We also collected a battery of demographic data (see table 1 below).

Follow-Up Interview Data

We conducted nineteen follow-up interviews with participants who agreed to be contacted by the research team following the dialogue. The interviews took place over the phone and in person two to four weeks after the election, and ten to twelve weeks after the dialogues. Each interviewer followed the predetermined protocol (see appendix D).

Analytic Approach

Data analysis included two approaches: first, we analyzed the quantitative survey data, generating simple descriptive statistics and disaggregating by various demographic groups to identify patterns by item, category, and participant. Second, we used an inductive coding method to analyze data from the interviews, building on an existing coding scheme developed during an initial review of interview data. Two coders shared the coding duties and maintained consistent communication to ensure reliability.

A Note on Methods and Sample

Before sharing the findings from the study, we feel it is important to address two potential methodological limitations. First, our sample was comprised entirely of volunteers, and the small sample size precluded us from creating control or experimental groups. Therefore, our participants necessarily were self-selected and therefore more likely to enter the dialogues with strongly held political beliefs (Barabas 2004). Although this trend certainly biases our sample in certain specific ways (e.g., strength of political beliefs and level of education), we believe that it does not negate our most compelling findings. Because we are interested in examining specifically how deliberation may impact participants' knowledge and attitudes about affirmative action, we argue that one's predisposition to attend a community dialogue does not inherently make one more (or less) likely to learn new information or gain understanding from it.

The second potential methodological limitation arises from the analysis of data that is primarily self-reported. To reduce potential limitations stemming from the use of self-reported data—including the threat of social desirability, or participants' inclination to respond in ways they perceive desirable to other participants and researchers (Fisher 1993; Nederhof 1985)—questionnaires were designed with multiple measures of participant attitudes. The inclusion of multiple measures allowed us to crosscheck participant knowledge and beliefs to examine the possibility that participants self-inflated their attitudinal responses to seem more "tolerant" or "inclusive" than they really are. Analyses revealed a heterogeneous distribution of participant attitudes—pre and post; this suggests that these concerns should not have significant impact on the interpretation of our results.

The sample of dialogue participants was somewhat diverse, varying in age, sex, race, education level, and income level. Table 1 shows the demographics of the participants.

The participants were predominantly white (58 percent), young (51 percent under thirty-five), female (62 percent), well educated (41 percent with a graduate degree), and not especially wealthy (67 percent making under $75,000 a year). This profile is not surprising, as a majority of the dialogue sessions took place in Boulder County, Colorado, in or near a college town with a highly educated (56.6 percent of Boulder County residents have a BA degree or higher; United States Census Bureau 2010), mostly white population (79.4 percent of Boulder County residents are white, non-Hispanic; United States Census Bureau 2010).

Questionnaires

Using the raw questionnaire data, we calculated a number of statistics related to our research questions. The true/false question responses provide an indicator of participants' affirmative action knowledge, both before (pre T/F score) and after (post T/F score) the dialogue. To calculate participants'

Table 1 Forum participant demographics

Age	N	Percent
18–24	15	19.0
25–34	25	31.6
35–44	15	19.0
45–54	6	7.6
55–64	5	6.3
65 and older	13	16.5
Gender		
Female	49	62.0
Male	29	36.7
No response	1	1.3
Race		
Asian American	2	2.5
Black, non-Latino	6	7.6
Latino	16	20.3
White, non-Latino	46	58.2
Other	4	5.1
No response	5	6.3
Education		
Some high school	1	1.3
High school degree	1	1.3
Some college	12	15.2
Associate's (AA) degree	1	1.3
Bachelor's degree	15	19.0
Some graduate school	17	21.5
Graduate degree	32	40.5
Income		
Less than 25,000	21	26.6
25,000–49,999	12	15.2
50,000–74,999	20	25.3
75,000–99,999	10	12.7
100,000–149,999	9	11.4
150,000 or greater	6	7.6
No response	1	1.3

"change in knowledge," we subtracted their pre from their post scores. We also used a series of eight Likert-scale questions (scaled 1 to 5) related to participant attitudes toward affirmative action. These questions provided a rough measure of any shift in attitude following the dialogue. Participants' post-dialogue attitude score minus the pre-dialogue attitude score yield a total "beliefs change" score. We also wanted a measurement that captured whether participants had any shift in the direction of their attitude (positive or negative) toward affirmative action, rather than the more nuanced measure captured by "beliefs change." To calculate this statistic (attitude change), we collapsed the negative and positive response categories to just one negative category and one positive category, leaving a neutral middle category. Therefore, the response range for the calculated *"attitude change"* variable is -1 to 1.

Results

Table 2 shows the means and standard deviations for each of these five calculated variables by demographic groups (and familiarity with affirmative action). Note that some groups have been omitted or collapsed due to small sample size (and to maintain confidentiality), and that total *N*s do not always equal 79, due to missing responses.

A number of patterns emerge from these data. Based on the questionnaires, we focus primarily on three areas of change among participants: affirmative action knowledge, attitudes toward affirmative action, and political participation and decision making. Below we briefly examine the evidence on each.

Affirmative Action Knowledge

In general, dialogue participants came very knowledgeable about affirmative action. This is evident in the questionnaire data, with the typical participant able to correctly answer roughly five out of seven questions about affirmative action policies, rules, and constitutional limitations (4.99 mean pre-knowledge score out of possible 7); this was also confirmed in our interview data. Many participants came to the dialogues because affirmative action was a policy about which they were particularly passionate.

Among pre-dialogue knowledge scores, women outscored men and people of color tended to outscore whites (whose scores were the lowest). These results suggest that the individuals most affected by a policy (in this case, racial minorities and women) tend to know the most about it. Participants with bachelor's degrees outscore both those with some college and those with graduate degrees. Finally, in our sample, pre-questionnaire affirmation action knowledge had a positive relationship with income (i.e., participants with higher incomes tended to correctly answer, on average, more questions about affirmative action) and an inverse relationship with age (i.e., younger participants tended to score higher than older participants).

These patterns shift when we examine the "knowledge change" scores, which indicate the participants' average growth in affirmative action knowledge over the course of the dialogues session. Men showed larger gains

Table 2 Changes in knowledge, beliefs, and attitudes about affirmative action

N		Pre T/F score		Post T/F score		Knowledge change		Beliefs change		Attitude change	
		Mean	SD	Mean	SD	Mean	SD	Mean	SD	Mean	SD
Income											
Less than 25,000	21	4.52	1.44	5.20	1.15	.50	1.10	1.73	3.02	1.11	2.35
25,000–49,999	12	5.08	1.51	5.33	1.30	.25	1.14	1.33	4.62	0.58	2.31
50,000–74,999	20	5.06	1.43	4.50	1.70	−.28	0.75	0.45	3.00	0.15	1.66
75,000–99,999	10	5.33	1.00	5.60	0.97	.44	0.73	−1.00	2.58	−0.50	2.59
100,000 or greater	15	5.27	1.37	5.21	1.38	−0.21	0.94	−0.36	2.41	−0.43	1.28
Education											
> Bachelor's degree	15	4.60	1.24	5.00	1.36	0.40	0.99	1.61	3.93	0.85	2.97
Bachelor's (or more)	32	5.19	1.47	5.47	0.97	0.10	0.86	0.52	3.40	0.19	1.92
Graduate degree	32	4.97	1.30	4.78	1.52	0.00	0.98	0.16	2.67	0.09	1.78
Race											
People of color[a]	24	5.67	1.01	5.88	.90	0.21	0.67	0.94	3.90	.32	2.36
White, non-Latino	46	4.56	1.35	4.66	1.38	0.12	1.05	0.42	3.03	.27	2.05
Gender											
Female	49	5.35	1.08	5.18	1.24	0.00	0.92	0.65	3.04	.12	1.91
Male	29	4.45	1.59	5.00	1.44	0.37	0.93	0.43	3.63	.54	2.39
Age											
18–24	15	5.07	1.22	5.33	1.29	0.27	1.03	1.84	3.96	.93	2.92
25–34	25	5.28	1.10	5.48	1.00	0.20	0.76	0.76	3.00	.40	1.61
35–44	15	5.21	1.72	5.21	1.63	−0.23	1.09	−0.53	3.70	−.40	2.59
45–64	11	4.64	1.69	4.90	1.10	0.10	1.20	0.22	1.30	−.22	0.44
65 and older	13	4.27	1.10	4.08	1.32	0.18	0.75	0.23	2.89	.38	1.76
Familiarity with affirmative action											
Not familiar	6	3.67	1.37	3.83	1.60	.17	1.47	1.60	4.35	1.20	3.83
Familiar	73	5.10	1.31	5.20	1.25	.12	.89	.48	3.13	.20	1.92
Total	79	4.99	1.36	5.09	1.32	.12	.94	.57	3.22	.26	2.07

[a]Including respondents who self-identified as Asian American, black, and Latino. Respondents who selected "other" or who declined to answer were not included in this portion of the analysis.

than women, which is not surprising given their lower pre-questionnaire scores. Interestingly, however, despite outscoring white participants on the pre-questionnaire, people of color posted slightly larger average gains than their white counterparts. In other words, the differences in affirmative action knowledge between white participants and participants of color *widened* following the dialogues. This connects back to the idea that those affected by a policy would know more about the issue and perhaps want to *add* to their knowledge about it more intensely than those who do not see themselves as personally affected. Furthermore, participants with less education (i.e., less than a bachelor's degree) showed the largest gains, and those with graduate degrees did not show any measurable change, on average.

Affirmative Action Beliefs and Attitudes

Dialogue participants did come with varying beliefs about affirmative action. By summing the strength of responses on the eight Likert-scale questions (scaled 1 to 5) related to participant attitudes toward affirmative action, participants were each assigned an index of attitudes toward affirmative action, ranging from 5 (the lowest possible score) to 40 (the highest possible score); in general, lower total scores are associated with more negative feelings about affirmative action. In our sample, the actual data yielded attitude scores ranging from 14 to 40 on the pre-questionnaire and 19 to 40 on the post-questionnaire, meaning the individuals with the most negative feelings about affirmative action—those with the minimum score of 14— were likely moved in a more positive direction. Further, the mean change across all participants was 0.57, a small positive increase in attitudes toward affirmative action. While this mean shift may not be practically significant, we do see some patterns of change that could represent a meaningful shift in attitudes toward affirmative action. Individuals making less than $25,000 a year, Latinos, participants aged eighteen to twenty-four, and those who were relatively unfamiliar with affirmative action prior to the forums all experienced positive changes in their beliefs about affirmative action (greater than 1.50 increase on the scale).

Interestingly, when participants were asked to self-report how the dialogue session affected their attitudes and beliefs toward affirmative action on the post-questionnaire, 48.6 percent reported that they felt exactly the same as they had prior to attending the forum; 45.9 percent reported that they felt either much more positive or slightly more positive than they had prior to attendance, and only 5.1 percent reported feeling slightly more negative toward affirmative action. This suggests—in conjunction with the small positive changes seen in the attitudinal index—that participants may have left with an overall improved attitude toward affirmative action programs, even if that general shift was not largely seen in the attitudinal index.

Political Participation and Decision Making

Participants indicated that they learned new information and perspectives because of the dialogues. More than half of all participants reported that their views on affirmative action changed; 16 percent said they were "much more positive" toward affirmative action after participating in the dialogue.

This pattern holds regardless of how knowledgeable participants were about affirmative action, the extent of their knowledge growth, or the reported quality of their deliberative experience. In participant interviews, few indicated that the dialogue caused them to *change* their vote on Amendment 46, but more than a third of participants stated that their dialogue participation had impacted their vote in some way.

In interviews, participants also indicated that they discussed their dialogue experiences with others: this sharing included discussion of both the policy-related and deliberation-related aspects of the forum. For example, one participant described leading her extended family in a lively discussion about Amendment 46, as a result of her experience in the dialogue. Another participant mentioned her intent to initiate a series of deliberative dialogues in her own community. These examples provide some evidence toward the claim that the impact of these dialogues does not end when the formal deliberation ends. Their impact may be diffuse and spreading and, admittedly, hard to pinpoint. It is apparent, however, that the dialogue participants were not the only people affected.

While participants on the whole rated their deliberative experiences favorably, it is unclear how likely such an experience is to promote further deliberation on policy issues. The mean agreement score for the statement "I will engage in more deliberation about policy issues in the future" was 3.89 on a scale of 1 to 5. White participants were least likely to agree with this statement, although the difference between their mean score and the general population of participants is quite small (with mean scores 3.76 and 3.89, respectively). Nevertheless, this result is somewhat curious, given that whites were *most* likely to agree that they had learned new information during the dialogue that helped shape their views on affirmative action. In fact, among all racial groups, there is a significant positive correlation between these two questions ($r=.25$, $p=.03$): the higher an individual rates the first question (new information), the higher he or she rates the second question (engage in deliberation). Therefore, according to participant self-reports, learning new information about the policy does lead individuals to alter their stance on affirmative action.

Values, Knowledge, and Deliberation

Taken together, the findings suggest that the community dialogue experience allowed participants to deliberate about important concepts like equality. They might not have come to agreement, but they were able to discuss the concepts as central to understandings about and rationalizations for affirmative action, perhaps coming away with a sense of the complexity of the issues involved with the policy. As one participant who entered the dialogue as an opponent to affirmative action shared, "that [dialogue] did open up my mind to how the other side felt on this particular issue." Participants were more knowledgeable about the legal underpinnings of affirmative action policy as well after taking part in the sessions. We also found that after deliberating with fellow citizens during the community dialogue, a majority of participants reported a more favorable view of affirmative action policy, like one woman who said, "what I've rethought is that it [affirmative action] has a purpose—a point, and it actually is making a difference and it's helpful." She went on to vote against Amendment 46 even though she had planned to vote for it at the start of the community dialogue session. Participants also reported that the dialogue experience served to galvanize group views, particularly when a strong majority favored affirmative action within a particular dialogue session. In addition, although most participants had an overall positive attitude toward affirmative action, they had a less positive attitude when asked questions specifically about Colorado. Participants were also the least knowledgeable about specific affirmative action policies in Colorado, even if they were knowledgeable about affirmative action in general. In addition, we noted—both in our experiences as facilitators and in follow-up analysis of dialogue videos and transcripts— the power of dialogue participants with perceived expertise; even when the information shared by a participant with perceived expertise was incorrect, other participants seemed to pay strong attention to and internalize the information (see Davidson and Moses 2012). Finally, findings from follow-up interviews suggest that a majority of our interview participants voted to preserve affirmative action in Colorado, regardless of whether they entered the community dialogue session with negative or favorable views about affirmative action. More than one-third of participants also reported that their vote was impacted directly by their participation in the dialogue.

Our data on political participation and decision making suggest that these processes are too complex to be captured by a few survey or interview questions. Participants believe that the dialogues were helpful as they considered the question posed by Amendment 46. A few even changed their intended vote as a result. Yet the mechanism at work is hard to tease out. What exactly pushes people to reconsider their views? Research-based information? Hearing others' perspectives and stories? Revisiting their own deeply held assumptions? We are inclined to think it is some combination of at least these three ideas (see Davidson and Moses 2012). And while the exact impacts of the dialogues remain unclear, it is clear that participants felt pushed to think more deeply about the issue, even if they came into the experience with firm beliefs.

Several findings point to the difficulties that arise when attempting to put deliberative principles into action. Despite the relative demographic diversity of our participant sample, our numbers were small and the majority of our participants came into the dialogues with a positive attitude about affirmative action. It was rare to find more than one or two individuals in a dialogue with strong beliefs against the policy. Though we strove to be as inclusive as possible, the reality was that affirmative action supporters were those most attracted to the dialogues in the first place. Most troubling is the fact that participants' prior level of support for affirmative action is positively correlated with the quality of their deliberative experience ($r=.34$, $p=.02$). That is, affirmative action supporters had a more positive experience than those with negative views on the policy. This finding was corroborated in interviews with participants, where it became clear that one major impact of the dialogues was to reinforce or galvanize preexisting beliefs about affirmative action. This galvanizing effect, identified by David Schkade, Cass Sunstein, and Reid Hastie (2006) as "ideological amplification" (917), can seriously impact the deliberative aspect of the dialogue. Not only do participants in the majority take fewer risks due to the comfort factor, those in the minority can feel attacked or singled out (Davidson and Moses 2012).

Conclusion

This research highlights how public dialogue can contribute to increased public information within a sociopolitical context where voters increasingly have opportunities to weigh in on deep moral disagreements and make policy decisions related to social equality issues via ballot initiative. Deliberative democratic theory is a kind of political theory that is designed to respond to the marked value pluralism that characterizes contemporary democratic societies. It places special emphasis on inclusive and fair participation in the process of political decision making (Benhabib 1996; Cohen 1997; Gutmann and Thompson 1996). Part of good deliberation is gaining a nuanced understanding of the nature of disagreements, the moral ideals involved, and the political commitments invoked. Gutmann and Thompson's (1996) framework is characterized by discussions and deliberations in which people publicly provide reasons and justifications for their views and decisions in a way that is broadly accessible. People need to hear both data-related and values-related information about disputed policies. As Lorraine McDonnell (2004) observes, "Even when potential targets disagree with a policy's goals and underlying values, if they at least share an understanding of it, debate and opposition can proceed in a thoughtful manner" (198). Our community dialogues showed that in their understanding of affirmative action, participants repeatedly invoked competing goods associated with the ideals of equality and liberty (Davidson and Moses 2012). As a participant explained, "sure, it feels unfair, you know, if I have equal qualifications and a minority person gets a position and I don't. Of course, I personally am going to feel like that was unfair, and perhaps that's a hardship for me. But, I'm willing to say, 'You know what, it's not just about me. It's what's been going on for generations.'"

Importantly, we as a research community can influence decision makers, as Clive Belfield and Henry Levin (2005) point out:

> Difficult decisions must be made about the appropriate trade-offs, and we predict that it is extremely hard to reach a consensus where philosophical differences are so strongly embedded in the opposing influences of libertarian and social contract perspectives. In our view this does not excuse researchers from the imperative for research that meets high methodological standards, and which others can replicate. Most important, this research should aim to be comprehensive in addressing all four criteria of freedom of choice, efficiency, equity, and social cohesion, presuming that there is still some audience whom evidence will sway, even given a strong set of prior values. (563)

Conducting strong research is one way to improve the deliberative quality of education policy debates. In addition, democratic deliberation by way of community dialogues allows citizens to voice their thoughts, concerns, beliefs, and arguments publicly, to hear alternative perspectives, and to consider policy in light of its effect on others or on a community. Deliberative dialogues also hold the potential to be educational spaces in which citizens learn more about controversial hot-button issues such as affirmative action: the history and context of affirmative action, the moral arguments for and against the policy, and research-based evidence regarding the effects of affirmative action. Well-informed citizens are likely to be well-informed voters, who in turn are likely to make well-reasoned and deliberative decisions about education policy. As Belfield and Levin (2005) also point out, however, even in the presence of strong evidence, individuals often turn to ideology or prior moral reasoning to judge policies. This indicates that individuals often may be more influenced by appeals to morality than by appeals to facts and evidence. This highlights the need for dialogue in order to better understand and stress common moral values, relationships, and ideals so as to render policy debates and decisions more thoughtful and complete.

Based on our experiences, we provide a number of suggestions for improving the quality of future community dialogues. These recommendations are designed to promote an inclusive, educative, and positive experience for participants.

1. Provide participants with specific, factual information; this includes stepping in to correct any misconceptions that arise or to answer questions that participants ask. This requires, of course, that facilitators be sufficiently knowledgeable to recognize such instances and be able to respond. In one of our dialogues, a participant with perceived authoritative knowledge offered a factually incorrect statement that appears to have "miseducated" the other participants. Facilitators should have the knowledge and authority to be able to intervene in such cases.

2. Ensure that minority viewpoints are heard and discussed. It is important to include all participants in the dialogue; therefore, facilitators should emphasize the purpose of the dialogue as *deliberation* rather than *consensus*. Group dynamics, as we saw, can lead to the reinforcing of already held views. While this in itself is not a negative outcome, it is possible that it can lead participants to dismiss or ignore alternative perspectives.

3. Cast a wide net: the more diversity you have among participants, the more likely you are to include multiple perspectives. Take advantage of preexisting groups that share things in common aside from ideological viewpoints, such as churches, neighborhood groups, and book clubs. We found that dialogues with groups such as these tended to generate lively discussion.

4. It is necessary, if we want to understand the impact of this deliberative activity, to follow up with participants many years down the road. For participants who carry the deliberative principles forward in their lives, there may be ripple effects about which we can only hypothesize. More research is needed, on this project and others, to determine how dialogue participants' lives are affected by their structured, deliberative experiences.

Our experiences tell us that deliberative community dialogues on controversial political issues are not merely possible; they foster an informed, participatory democracy. The model we used can serve as a framework for future deliberative dialogues, and we can continue to refine the model to make it more inclusive and useful for citizens who wish to be more informed in their political life. Our results affirm that small-group dialogues across different groups can contribute to participants' greater information and understanding about a given controversial education policy issue, in this case affirmative action.

With this in mind, in the next chapter, I return more centrally to the idea of moral disagreement and what it means for race-conscious education policy. I conclude with a complex story about how moral disagreement may enhance democratic participation even as it is frustrating and difficult—or impossible—to resolve. I argue that scholars ought to view the deep moral disagreements about education policy as opportunities to take on more active roles in providing evidence-based information to the public. Such education, in combination with opportunities for public deliberation about controversial matters of education policy holds promise in the quest for greater respect and mutual understanding in the face of seemingly intractable moral disagreements.

SIX

What Should We Do about Profound Moral Disagreements over Education Policy?

Chapter 3 quotes Glenn Loury (2002) as saying that the controversy over affirmative action does not hinge on facts and, as such, would not be resolved by appeals to evidence. In a way, my arguments in this book are responding to this kind of claim. Although I agree with Loury on this point, as an education scholar and researcher concerned with providing and using evidence to inform policy decisions, I was spurred to write this book because it did not seem accurate to imply that we cannot make progress on a resolution to the moral disagreement about race-conscious education policies like affirmative action. I wanted to understand more deeply the nature of the enduring disagreement; I wanted to understand the possibilities for a way forward. In the end, Loury's words ring true, but I do have hope about the possibilities—maybe not of *resolution*, but of greater understanding and more democratic participation. Profound disagreements do not need to be polarizing fodder for fights; they can serve to stimulate discussion and understanding, cause people to refine their views and concomitant policy solutions, resist authoritarianism, and honor differences and pluralism. Eliminating moral disagreement is not necessarily desirable in that it may go too far in eliminating other important differences between people (Mouffe 2009). One alternative to addressing moral disagreements is surrendering to immoral means of resolving disputes (e.g., majority tyranny; see chapter 4). However, to the extent that everyone in a society wants the policies in that society to be moral and fair, there must be discussion about moral disagreements so that it can be understood why one side thinks one solution is moral while another side thinks the same solution is immoral.

Moral and political disagreements are inescapable parts of a liberal democratic society, as Isaiah Berlin (2000) reminds us:

We must say that the world in which what we see as incompatible values are not in conflict is a world altogether beyond our ken; that principles which are harmonized in this other world are not the principles with which, in our daily lives, we are acquainted; if they are transformed, it is into conceptions not known to us on earth. But it is on earth that we live, and it is here that we must believe and act. (199–200)

Such disagreements and conflicts seem to be, as well, inescapable parts of education policy. I used to think that moral disagreements about education policy could be resolved fully, if only we appealed reasonably and intelligently to common ground and shared ideals. My inquiry in this book shows that shared ideals do exist, but they may be interpreted in conflicting ways by opposing sides. When that happens, competing policy prescriptions may emerge despite the shared ideals. This is certainly the case with affirmative action policy. Other examples from education in addition to affirmative action policy include bilingual education, teacher education, and school choice policies. Even after the US Supreme Court has ruled on such topics, moral disagreements have remained; a real middle ground is difficult to find. But even if we accept that a number of moral disagreements in education policy will be intractable, where does that get us? After all, policy decisions still have to be made, so what do we *do*? Berlin (2000) asks a relevant question: if persistent, irreconcilable moral and political disagreement is inevitable in a democratic society, then, "'What is to be done?' How do we choose between possibilities?" And he answers: "There is, it seems to me, no clear reply" (202). Somehow democratic citizens need to learn to cope with the idea that there indeed may be "no clear reply." One thing that I have learned from the inquiry I undertook for this book is that those of us concerned with just education policies on controversial issues ought to think about striving for a balance between finding common ground and respecting differences, while also being able to take a stand for what one believes is morally right, grounded in important democratic ideals.

As examined in the previous chapters, based on the possibilities for mutual understanding and even compromise that come from the very fact of having some shared ideals, as well as the promise of deliberative dialogue, I argue that we need to learn to accept the disagreements themselves as an inevitable part of a pluralist democratic society. Simply put, there is an important lesson in "living with moral disagreement": moral disagreements about policy reveal the necessity of democratic politics.[1] As such, scholars, researchers, and educators should approach the moral disagreements over controversial education policies as opportunities to be active in the community, provide public information, and foster democratic deliberation. I argue further that education scholars have an important role to play in helping citizens grapple with the moral disagreement.

Pluralism

My argument comes out of pluralist deliberative democratic theory. Pluralist deliberative democrats seek "the fairest terms of living with a recalcitrant pluralism," as opposed to consensual deliberative democrats, who believe that "deliberation [should] aim at achieving consensus through realizing a common good" (26). The way Gutmann and Thompson (2004) explain it, pluralist deliberative democrats,

> drawing on the liberal tradition, argue that it is not always desirable to seek a comprehensive common good rather than to try to live respectfully with moral disagreements. One reason, they pointed out, is that some of these disagreements are inherent in the human condition. They arise because of our incomplete and incompatible moral and empirical understandings. (27)

Because disagreements function also to contribute strength and vitality to democratic society, we ought to seek greater understanding of and (when appropriate) respect for reasonable views instead of consensus around a particular view all the time. Opportunities for democratic deliberation are crucial in this regard. Such opportunities tend to affect participants' perspectives so that they come to view controversial issues less from a purely personal perspective and more from a community perspective (Melville, Willingham, and Dedrick 2005). In thinking about fair policies, this move from the personal to the ethical (Nagel 1991) is a crucial piece in the equitable and moral social and political treatment of others. Dialogue and deliberation, I contend, contribute to such a progression; dialogue is key to transforming and expanding people's views, as it "sinks into our bones and is remembered" (Zetzer 2005, 4). Even so, we should not expect dialogue participants to find more common ground or social unity after such dialogue experiences; however, that is not necessarily a negative outcome, especially when the conversations are rich with meaningful discussions about difference and conflicting values and perspectives (Walsh 2007). Similarly, as Gutmann and Thompson (2004) point out, "Deliberation cannot make incompatible values compatible. . . . [I]t can help participants recognize the moral merit in their opponents' claims when those claims have merit. It can also help deliberators distinguish those disagreements that arise from genuinely incompatible values from those that can be more resolvable than they first appear" (11). Most important, dialogues have to be inclusive; organizers and facilitators have to be well trained to care for all participants so that none of them feel excluded, silenced, or exploited within the dialogue process (Ellsworth 1989).

Mutual Respect and Compromise

A central aim of the kinds of democratic dialogue for which I am advocating is for *mutual* learning and transformation to occur. This is quite different from, say, one group of people urging another group to take up their (oftentimes minority) perspectives or a conversation in which more privileged participants learn from marginalized participants' painful experiences with oppression (Ellsworth 1989). Participants need dispositions such as mutual respect and mutual recognition so that the dialogue is set up for all participants to learn from others and expand their information and perspectives. I am thinking here of Green's (1998) ideas about the importance of developing "egalitarian solidarity" (186):

> It is the disposition to ally oneself with others not because they are similar to oneself in social background or agree with one's own tastes and values but precisely because they are different *and yet* have permanently common human interests. It is the mutual recognition of *these* interests, not the mere recognition of being in the same economic or social position, that defines solidarity among equals. Without this sense of mutual recognition, as well as the sentiment of empathy that underlies it, a mass politics of resentment is possible but egalitarian politics is not. (187)

Disagreement—the fact that we can have it and talk about it—can be thought of as fundamentally democratic, that is, part of what makes a democracy vibrant, tolerant, and open minded. A relevant example in this vein comes from US Supreme Court Justice John Paul Stevens. Unlike other justices who tend to be more concerned with consensus, he believes in the importance of highlighting the dissent within the court. This is in direct contrast to what he sees as the danger of squelching disagreement in favor of the *appearance* of unity and consensus (Rosen 2007; Walsh 2007).

In cases where there seems to be more than one possible "right" answer, depending on one's underlying values and theory of justice, it would make more sense to strive for deeper understanding and mutual respect between perspectives. According to Gutmann and Thompson (2004), "Mutual respect among those who reasonably disagree is *a value in itself*, and in turn it has further beneficial effect for democratic politics" (134, emphasis added). Indeed, the process of getting to greater understanding of one another's views, of learning to regard the other with greater respect, is key to a healthy democracy that can function well in the face of moral disagreement (Appiah 2006; Shook 2013). In a similar vein, I want to point out that there can be positive outcomes from the existence of moral disagreements including the opportunity to engage deeply with one's own beliefs and values as well as the ideas of others, and learn together in common humanity (Mason 1993, 146). Related to the ideas presented in chapter 5, there is promising evidence that as a result of participation in deliberative democratic forums, individual participants: (1) develop a "heightened interest in specific issues and in public affairs" leading to higher levels of public engagement; (2) broaden their perspective; (3) "come to experience themselves in different ways, and . . . learn new ways of taking part in groups"; (4) gain an enhanced "sense of themselves as political actors who can make a difference in their communities"; (5) expand their idea of their self-interest; and (6) transcend "superficial preferences to considered public judgment." (Melville, Willingham, and Dedrick 2005, 48–50). In these ways, disagreement—and dialogue and deliberation about the disagreement—serve an important democratic function (Sunstein 1996). Discussion, debate, dialogue, argument, communication, storytelling, and reason giving are the core of democratic participation and deliberation (Young 1996, 2000). In addition, Gutmann and Thompson (2004) explain that working toward mutual respect "requires a favorable attitude toward, and constructive interaction with, the persons with whom one disagrees. It consists in a reciprocal positive regard of citizens who manifest the excellence of character that permits a democracy to flourish in the face of . . . irresolvable moral conflict" (79). Within deliberative democracy, then, individuals' ideas are taken into account, and they will be motivated to give mutually acceptable reasons for their views and perspectives.

Consider the idea of an integrity-preserving compromise (Benjamin 1990) as a way through the dichotomy of consensus and disagreement. This idea is promising because it is qualitatively different from seeking only full resolution or consensus and argues against the all too common practice of disputants digging their heels in and arguing until they are blue in the face without ever intending to budge on their positions. An integrity-preserving compromise goes beyond merely "agreeing to disagree" and promotes more democratic participation as citizens agree to communicate, discuss, deliberate, and understand. Berlin (2000) makes a relevant point: "[moral]

collisions, even if they cannot be avoided, can be softened. Claims can be balanced, compromises can be reached" (202). Political compromise that does not betray one's principles requires, according to Martin Benjamin (1990), "commitment, long hours of skillful coalition-building and negotiation, astute judgment, and a receptive social climate" (71). Even with such policy compromise, underlying moral disagreements will not necessarily dissipate. In a liberal democracy, that is appropriate within the overall democratic project. A policy decision is made—for now—and will be revisited.

Affirmative Action as an Example of an Intractable Policy

As I have argued herein, affirmative action is an important example of a moral disagreement about education policy that resists easy resolution. The following factors characterize the enduring disagreement about affirmative action policy: both sides of the affirmative action debate seem to hold reasonable moral positions, and they both "argue from different plausible premises to fundamentally conflicting public policies"[2] (Gutmann and Thompson 2004, 74). Opponents of affirmative action base their argument on the principles of both liberty and equality (and sometimes diversity). Proponents of affirmative action base their argument on the principles of equality and diversity (and sometimes liberty). Both sides can agree on the general moral principles, but their interpretations of what those concepts mean and require of policy often are different. In addition, both take into consideration seemingly sound research evidence to support their claims.[3] In shaping the policy landscape related to affirmative action, each central moral ideal (i.e., equality, liberty, diversity) has been shifted slightly to accommodate the others.

The profound and persistent disagreement about affirmative action in higher education and the concomitant revision of affirmative action policies has served to strengthen both the policy and democratic deliberation about the policy. Quotas have been struck down, as have arbitrary numerical set asides, and diversity as a compelling state interest has emerged as a strong justificatory concept. Equality and social justice remain other important justificatory concepts, as do remedying the present effects of past discrimination and strengthening the economy, although somewhat less publicly acceptable than the diversity rationale. Part of the reason is that the ideal of diversity seems to be viewed favorably by those on both sides of the political spectrum. So the dialogue and debate about affirmative action for the past half century have improved on the original vision and justification of the policy. Some would argue that the compromises have weakened the policy, especially as regards its social justice rationale (Bell 2003). This indeed may be the case, but a modified affirmative action policy might be a more publicly acceptable policy and perhaps a better policy so long as it does not lose sight of its goals to increase equality of educational opportunity and cultural diversity on campus. I want to be clear here that I am not saying that those who strongly support affirmative action should alter their principled convictions. What is important is that the give-and-take between reasonable views that shape or modify policy prescriptions has the potential to make the policy more publicly viable. This speaks to the type of integrity-preserving compromise that Benjamin (1990) had in mind.

Scholars and Public Deliberation

Scholars and researchers hold a unique place in the political landscape; they often have access to complex sources of information and a nuanced understanding of issues about which citizens may be interested but are not necessarily knowledgeable. In the case of race-conscious education policy, this is certainly true. Typical citizens rarely have access to, for example, recent research on the impact of Proposal 2 in Michigan or Initiative 424 in Nebraska, nor are they likely to have a solid understanding of affirmative action's philosophical roots or history (Moses and Saenz 2008). Experts in the field, which include scholars, researchers, educators, and policymakers, are deeply knowledgeable about these issues and have a responsibility to make that knowledge a part of public political information.

Given the conceptual, theoretical, and empirical arguments I have shared, I close with an argument compelling scholars to use their expertise in the service of public deliberation. Specifically, I recommend that education scholars make greater efforts to bring their expertise into the community and public arena through various venues, including public community dialogues. As one avenue to foster public deliberation, such dialogues are effective ways for scholars to engage with members of the public, share philosophically and empirically informed policy information as well as their expertise, and contribute to society's deliberative democratic aims. In this way they may be able to get closer to what Michael Eric Dyson (2003) suggests about scholars' public obligations: "knowledge must be turned to social benefit if we are to justify the faith placed in us" (B12). In the arena of race-conscious education policy, education theorists and policy researchers have a significant responsibility to contribute theoretical and empirical grounding for the information that members of the public receive as they attempt to understand and negotiate their way through some of the most contentious moral disagreements faced by society.

Conclusion

Have patience with everything unresolved in your heart and to try to love the questions themselves as if they were locked rooms or books written in a very foreign language. Don't search for the answers, which could not be given to you now, because you would not be able to live them. And the point is, to live everything. Live the questions now. Perhaps then, someday far in the future, you will gradually, without even noticing it, live your way into the answer.

—Rainer Maria Rilke ([1903] 2001, letter 4)

As Rilke advises, we need to love the questions themselves. Moral disagreements in US society are such that we will not be able to solve or resolve them all of the time. In response to the question of what should we do about that, I argue that we should understand how moral disagreements—although certainly frustrating and difficult—are an inevitable part of a vital, deliberative democratic society. In a sense, values conflicts are as Berlin (2000) explains, "the essence of . . . what we are," and they cannot be resolved easily as if we live in "some perfect world in which all good things can be harmonized in principle" (199).

As such, citizens ought to honor reasonable disagreements and the differences that underlie them. We should focus efforts on increasing understanding, trying to stand in others' shoes, fostering mutual respect, and working hard to attain worthy, integrity-preserving compromises. This requires dialogue, empathy, an ability to capitalize on the ideals we do share, and a consistent focus on deliberation. Dialogue and democratic deliberation hold great promise; they are not a "solution" to disagreement but a way of increasing information, hopefully understanding, perhaps respecting, and possibly achieving policy compromises. This may be all we ought to expect with such entrenched and deep-seated moral disagreements and different—opposing—moral worldviews. I hope this book has shed some light on the nature of the enduring moral disagreement about affirmative action that began before *Bakke* and continues. Perhaps more questions have been raised than answered, but in a democratic society, questions and deliberations can lead us to greater understanding and—I hope—more equitable policy decisions.

So, given general support for the democratic ideals of basic equality, liberty, and diversity, *can* we transcend profound moral disagreements about race-conscious education policies like affirmative action? This is a sobering question, especially because there seem to be myriad other examples of impossible moral conflicts. Consider the debates about abortion and euthanasia, the conflict between creationism and evolution, competing claims about the state's responsibility to people in poverty or undocumented workers; the list could go on. I am afraid that the answer is more complicated than a simple yes or no. I am not at all sure that we can always find common ground strong enough to allow widespread agreement on policy prescriptions. But what we can find are some common gateways to dialogue and understanding.

That a disagreement endures regarding the use of affirmative action to foster racial and ethnic diversity on college campuses as well as greater social equality should not cause advocates of equality of educational opportunity to hang their heads in defeat or despair. Those who care deeply about equality of educational opportunity and equity in educational access and outcomes can take advantage of the emphasis both supporters and opponents of affirmative action place on the important concepts analyzed in this book: equality, liberty, and diversity. We are much closer to having more widely acceptable versions of affirmative action in higher education admissions than when Justice Powell wrote his *Bakke* opinion. The Supreme Court gave more guidance with the *Gratz* and *Grutter* decisions. The salience of the diversity ideal shone through as a compelling state interest, but always in the service of the ideals of equality and liberty both.

Ultimately we need to keep trying, keep talking, and keep listening. It will be a long-term process to provide more information about controversial issues of moral disagreement and promote greater understanding and respect of different views. A crucial part of it is educating young people about moral disagreements differently than we have educated adults.[4] Perhaps above all, this will hold the key to better understanding and transcending the impasses. In the spirit of non-ideal theory, it is important for citizens and residents to find acceptable ways of living with moral disagreement. As Berlin (2000) advises in the quotation at the beginning of this chapter: "it is on earth that we live, and it is here that we must believe and act" (200). Education scholars ought to share their expertise to inform people's beliefs and actions about education policies, in the service of promoting mutual respect as well as equality of educational opportunity, richly understood.

Pre-Questionnaire

Demographic Information

1. Age
   ___ 18–24
   ___ 25–34
   ___ 35–44
   ___ 45–54
   ___ 55–64
   ___ 65 and older

2. Gender
   ___ Female
   ___ Male

3. In what city/town is your primary residence?

4. Please select the race/ethnicity with which you identify. Choose as many as apply.
   ___ Asian or Pacific Islander
   ___ American Indian or Alaskan Native
   ___ Black, non-Latino
   ___ Latino
   ___ White, non-Latino
   ___ Other, please specify:
   ___ Prefer not to say

5. What is your highest level of educational attainment?
   ___ Some high school
   ___ High school degree

___ Some college

___ Associate's (AA) degree

___ Bachelor's degree

___ Some graduate school

___ Graduate degree

Please specify:

6. What is your average annual household income?

    ___ Less than $25,000

    ___ $25,000—$49,999

    ___ $50,000—$74,999

    ___ $75,000—$99,999

    ___ $100,000—$149,999

    ___ $150,000 or greater

Affirmative Action Knowledge

1. Were you familiar with affirmative action prior to coming to this forum?

    ___ No

    ___ Yes, familiar with

2. If you were familiar with affirmative action prior to this forum, please indicate the sources from which you learned about it. Select all that apply.

    ___ Newspapers (online or print)

    ___ Television news reports

    ___ Blogs

    ___ Friends/family

    ___ Magazines

    ___ In a class/informational session

    ___ Other, please describe:

3. What are the arguments in support of affirmative action in higher education? List as many as you can think of.

4. What are the arguments against affirmative action in higher education? List as many as you can think of.

Please mark the following statements True (T) or False (F).

    ___ 1. According to the Supreme Court, the constitution allows for the consideration of a student's race or ethnicity among other factors in college admissions.

    ___ 2. Affirmative action allows colleges or universities to set quotas to admit a certain number of minority students.

___ 3. In Colorado, colleges and universities are allowed to award extra points to an applicant if he or she is a member of an underrepresented minority group.

___ 4. Affirmative action has not succeeded in increasing female and minority representation.

___ 5. Affirmative action is legal in some states, but not others.

___ 6. Banning affirmative action has little to no effect on the admissions and enrollment of minority students.

___ 7. Support for affirmative action means support for preferential selection procedures that favor unqualified candidates over qualified candidates.

Affirmative Action Beliefs

For each of the following statements, please indicate the strength to which you agree or disagree.

1. Affirmative action in our state universities and colleges is a necessary policy tool.

___ Strongly disagree

___ Disagree

___ Neutral

___ Agree

___ Strongly agree

2. Affirmative action unfairly discriminates against white people.

___ Strongly disagree

___ Disagree

___ Neutral

___ Agree

___ Strongly agree

3. Affirmative action is the same as preferential treatment.

___ Strongly disagree

___ Disagree

___ Neutral

___ Agree

___ Strongly agree

4. Public universities and colleges should be allowed to consider a student's race or ethnicity if they believe it is important.

___ Strongly disagree

___ Disagree

___ Neutral

___ Agree

___ Strongly agree

5. An individual's race or ethnicity impacts the way he or she experiences higher education.

___ Strongly disagree

___ Disagree

___ Neutral

___ Agree

___ Strongly agree

6. An individual's race or ethnicity has no bearing on his or her educational experiences.

___ Strongly disagree

___ Disagree

___ Neutral

___ Agree

___ Strongly agree

7. A racially and ethnically diverse student body is something Colorado's colleges and universities should try to achieve.

___ Strongly disagree

___ Disagree

___ Neutral

___ Agree

___ Strongly agree

8. Affirmative action is a good way to achieve a racially and ethnically diverse student body.

___ Strongly disagree

___ Disagree

___ Neutral

___ Agree

___ Strongly agree

Post-Questionnaire

Affirmative Action Knowledge

1. What are the arguments in support of affirmative action in higher education? List as many as you can think of.

2. What are the arguments against affirmative action in higher education? List as many as you can think of.

Please mark the following statements True (T) or False (F).

___ 1. According to the Supreme Court, the constitution allows for the consideration of a student's race or ethnicity among other factors in college admissions.

___ 2. Affirmative action allows colleges or universities to set quotas to admit a certain number of minority students.

___ 3. In Colorado, colleges and universities are allowed to award extra points to an applicant if he or she is a member of an underrepresented minority group.

___ 4. Affirmative action has not succeeded in increasing female and minority representation.

___ 5. Affirmative action is legal in some states, but not others.

___ 6. Banning affirmative action has little to no effect on the admissions and enrollment of minority students.

___ 7. Support for affirmative action means support for preferential selection procedures that favor unqualified candidates over qualified candidates.

Affirmative Action Beliefs

Indicate the strength to which you agree or disagree with the following statements.

1. Affirmative action in our state universities and colleges is a necessary policy tool.

____ Strongly disagree

____ Disagree

____ Neutral

____ Agree

____ Strongly agree

2. Affirmative action unfairly discriminates against white people.

____ Strongly disagree

____ Disagree

____ Neutral

____ Agree

____ Strongly agree

3. Affirmative action is the same as preferential treatment.

____ Strongly disagree

____ Disagree

____ Neutral

____ Agree

____ Strongly agree

4. Public universities and colleges should be allowed to consider a student's race or ethnicity if they believe it is important.

____ Strongly disagree

____ Disagree

____ Neutral

____ Agree

____ Strongly agree

5. An individual's race or ethnicity impacts the way he or she experiences higher education.

____ Strongly disagree

____ Disagree

____ Neutral

____ Agree

____ Strongly agree

6. An individual's race or ethnicity has no bearing on his or her educational experiences.

____ Strongly disagree

____ Disagree

___ Neutral

___ Agree

___ Strongly agree

7. A racially and ethnically diverse student body is something Colorado's colleges and universities should try to achieve.

___ Strongly disagree

___ Disagree

___ Neutral

___ Agree

___ Strongly agree

8. Affirmative action is a good way to achieve a racially and ethnically diverse student body.

___ Strongly disagree

___ Disagree

___ Neutral

___ Agree

___ Strongly agree

Deliberation Experience

1. After participating in this forum, my views about affirmative action are:

___ Exactly the same as before

___ Much more positive toward affirmative action policies

___ Slightly more positive toward affirmative action policies

___ Slightly more negative toward affirmative action policies

___ Much more negative toward affirmative action policies

Indicate the strength to which you agree or disagree with the following statements.

2. I learned new information today that helped shape my view on affirmative action.

___ Strongly disagree

___ Disagree

___ Neutral

___ Agree

___ Strongly agree

3. I heard new perspectives today that helped shape my view on affirmative action.

___ Strongly disagree

___ Disagree

___ Neutral

___ Agree

___ Strongly agree

4. I feel better prepared to explain affirmative action to others.

___ Strongly disagree

___ Disagree

___ Neutral

___ Agree

___ Strongly agree

5. I am more knowledgeable about affirmative action than I was before.

___ Strongly disagree

___ Disagree

___ Neutral

___ Agree

___ Strongly agree

6. I felt comfortable sharing my ideas and opinions with the group.

___ Strongly disagree

___ Disagree

___ Neutral

___ Agree

___ Strongly agree

7. I will engage in more deliberation about policy issues in the future.

___ Strongly disagree

___ Disagree

___ Neutral

___ Agree

___ Strongly agree

8. I have a better understanding about the many sides to the affirmative action debate.

___ Strongly disagree

___ Disagree

___ Neutral

___ Agree

___ Strongly agree

Other Comments:

Post-Post-Questionnaire

Affirmative Action Knowledge

Please mark the following statements True (T) or False (F).

_____ 1. According to the Supreme Court, the constitution allows for the consideration of a student's race or ethnicity among other factors in college admissions.

_____ 2. Affirmative action allows colleges or universities to set quotas to admit a certain number of minority students.

_____ 3. In Colorado, colleges and universities are allowed to award extra points to an applicant if he or she is a member of an underrepresented minority group.

_____ 4. Affirmative action has not succeeded in increasing female and minority representation.

_____ 5. Affirmative action is legal in some states, but not others.

_____ 6. Banning affirmative action has little to no effect on the admissions and enrollment of minority students.

_____ 7. Support for affirmative action means support for preferential selection procedures that favor unqualified candidates over qualified candidates.

Affirmative Action Beliefs

Indicate the strength to which you agree or disagree with the following statements.

1. Affirmative action in our state universities and colleges is a necessary policy tool.

_____ Strongly disagree

_____ Disagree

_____ Neutral

___ Agree

___ Strongly agree

2. Affirmative action unfairly discriminates against white people.

___ Strongly disagree

___ Disagree

___ Neutral

___ Agree

___ Strongly agree

3. Affirmative action is the same as preferential treatment.

___ Strongly disagree

___ Disagree

___ Neutral

___ Agree

___ Strongly agree

4. Public universities and colleges should be allowed to consider a student's race or ethnicity if they believe it is important.

___ Strongly disagree

___ Disagree

___ Neutral

___ Agree

___ Strongly agree

5. An individual's race or ethnicity impacts the way he or she experiences higher education.

___ Strongly disagree

___ Disagree

___ Neutral

___ Agree

___ Strongly agree

6. An individual's race or ethnicity has no bearing on his or her educational experiences.

___ Strongly disagree

___ Disagree

___ Neutral

___ Agree

___ Strongly agree

7. A racially and ethnically diverse student body is something Colorado's colleges and universities should try to achieve.

___ Strongly disagree

___ Disagree

___ Neutral

___ Agree

___ Strongly agree

8. Affirmative action is a good way to achieve a racially and ethnically diverse student body.

___ Strongly disagree

___ Disagree

___ Neutral

___ Agree

___ Strongly agree

Deliberation Experience

1. Several weeks after the forum, my views about affirmative action are:

___ Exactly the same as before

___ Much more positive toward affirmative action policies

___ Slightly more positive toward affirmative action policies

___ Slightly more negative toward affirmative action policies

___ Much more negative toward affirmative action policies

Indicate the strength to which you agree or disagree with the following statements.

2. I learned new information at the forum that helped shape my view on affirmative action.

___ Strongly disagree

___ Disagree

___ Neutral

___ Agree

___ Strongly agree

3. I heard new perspectives at the forum that helped shape my view on affirmative action.

___ Strongly disagree

___ Disagree

___ Neutral

___ Agree

___ Strongly agree

4. I feel better prepared to explain affirmative action to others.

___ Strongly disagree

___ Disagree

___ Neutral

___ Agree

___ Strongly agree

5. I am more knowledgeable about affirmative action than I was before.

___ Strongly disagree

___ Disagree

___ Neutral

___ Agree

___ Strongly agree

6. I will engage in more deliberation about policy issues in the future.

___ Strongly disagree

___ Disagree

___ Neutral

___ Agree

___ Strongly agree

8. I have a better understanding about the many sides to the affirmative action debate.

___ Strongly disagree

___ Disagree

___ Neutral

___ Agree

___ Strongly agree

Other Comments:

Follow-Up Interview Protocol

[Follow-up interviews were conducted with individual dialogue participants who agree to be contacted for a follow-up interview. They took place by telephone approximately two months after the dialogue occurred.]

Questions

1. Did you feel more informed about issues related to affirmative action after participating in the deliberative forum? Can you provide an example of something that you learned?
2. Have you rethought your views about affirmative action since the forum? How so?
3. Did you talk with anyone not present at the forum about affirmative action issues? What did you share with them from the forums?
4. Did the community dialogue help you make your decision about how to vote on relevant ballot initiatives such as Amendment 46? How so?
5. If you feel comfortable, would you share with us how you voted on Amendment 46?
6. How did your forum experience affect the way you approached voting on other issues?

NOTES

CHAPTER ONE

1. See, e.g., Moses 2001, 2002, 2008, 2010.
2. I should note that I am aware that this is a contested term. All people have "color." I use the terms *students of color* and *people of color* to signify racialized people who currently are in the numerical minority overall in the United States, for lack of a term that better identifies this group.
3. The idea of opportunities "worth wanting" was conceptualized by Ken Howe (1997), based on Daniel Dennett's ideas in the book *Elbow Room* (1984).
4. I thank the manuscript reviewers for pointing this out to me.
5. A lengthy discussion of ideal and non-ideal theory is beyond the scope of this book. Please see the following sources for relevant analyses: Rawls 1971; Mills 2005; Moses 2015; Simmons 2010; Tessman 2009; Valentini 2012.
6. See, e.g., Moses 2002.

CHAPTER TWO

1. These cases are different from previous ones in that the plaintiffs are Asian American, which complicates discussions about race, discrimination, diversity, and social justice.
2. Also at the time of this writing, another affirmative action–related case was heard before the US Supreme Court: *Schuette v. Coalition to Defend Affirmative Action* (2014). And, as mentioned at the beginning of this chapter, two lawsuits involving challenges to affirmative action at Harvard University and University of North Carolina at Chapel Hill were filed in federal court in 2014. This moral disagreement is not going away anytime soon.
3. Although there are other cases related to affirmative action regarding K–12 education, as well as hiring and contracting decisions, an examination of those is beyond the scope of this chapter.
4. Much legal debate ensued after the Fifth Circuit issued this opinion. Some legal scholars argued that the Fifth Circuit did not have the authority to overrule the US Supreme Court (Torres 2003).
5. The Top Ten Percent Plan served as the model for the percent plans later implemented in California and Florida.

6. In O'Connor's words: "We expect that 25 years from now, the use of racial prefer-
    ences will no longer be necessary to further the interest approved today" (*Grutter*
    2003, 343).
7. Deardorff and Jones's (2007) survey of southern and midwestern colleges showed
    that among the southern schools, although administrators generally did not support
    or agree with the University of Michigan decisions, they all agreed that race plays a
    significant role in our society, and administrators at all schools reported that diver-
    sity was important.
8. These cases were combined by the US Supreme Court as *Parents Involved in Commu-
    nity Schools v. Seattle School District No. 1*, 551 U.S. 701 (2007).
9. In Oklahoma, the language of the initiative differed from the other five states.
10. Once passed, such legislation is very difficult to undo. The Supreme Court rulings in
    Gratz and *Grutter* set the parameters for what is constitutionally permissible; they did
    not overturn California's Proposition 209 or Washington's Initiative 200, which were
    political actions curbing affirmative action.
11. Because this chapter focuses on college and university admissions, I address SP-1,
    which eliminated affirmative action in UC admissions policy; SP-2, which elimi-
    nated affirmative action in UC hiring and contracting, was passed simultaneously
    but is not relevant for the discussion here.
12. I place "preferences" in scare quotes because it is a controversial term used predomi-
    nantly by those opposed to affirmative action. I do not interpret affirmative action as
    "preferences." In keeping with the ruling in *Grutter* (2003) and egalitarian political
    theory, I view race as one possible factor among many in the admissions process.

CHAPTER THREE

1. Only voters who indicated they were at least 70 percent confident they remember
    how they voted on Amendment 46 were included in the sample. The survey was
    terminated for all voters who indicated that they were less than 70 percent confident.
2. Participants were randomly sampled from a population stratified by eighteen
    regions, comprising sixty-four Colorado counties. The regions were made up of
    counties matched on general voting patterns (typically Democratic versus typically
    Republican counties), degree to which they were urban, and physical proximity to
    each other. All surveys were administered over the phone by Voter Consumer Re-
    search, an independent research company, in 2008. The full survey included ques-
    tions on voting behaviors, attitudes toward affirmative action, influences of various
    campaign activities and public media, and demographic information. Analyses of
    voter demographics (e.g., gender, race, political affiliation, income, and age) indi-
    cated that the sample was generally representative of Colorado voters. Of the re-
    spondents, 51.3 percent were female; 16.1 percent identified themselves as people
    of color, including 2 percent identifying as Native American/Alaskan Native, 1 per-
    cent identifying as Asian American/Pacific Islander, 4.3 percent identifying as His-
    panic/Latino, 2.4 percent identifying as Black/African American, and 6.5 percent
    identifying as Multiracial/Multiethnic; 35.1 percent identified as Republicans, 33.5
    percent as Democrats, 23.5 percent as Independents (7.9 percent either identified
    another party affiliation or refused to answer the question). Fifty-one percent re-
    ported voting for Barack Obama. The median age for respondents was fifty-two, with
    a range of eighteen to ninety-two years old; the median family income was $65,500,
    ranging from under $1,000 to $7 million. The sample was largely English speaking,
    as well. Spanish-speaking survey administrators were available, but only 1 percent of

respondents selected a language other than English as the primary language spoken at home.

3. Only 28.2 percent of respondents were able to articulate that the initiative would prohibit affirmative action policies; just over 5 percent stated that the amendment would protect affirmative action or equal opportunity policies; and the vast majority of voters (66.3 percent) restated the initiative in a way that did not allow us to determine the perceived impact of the initiative. In sum, few voters explicitly stated that Amendment 46 would preserve affirmative action; instead, the vast majority of responses were deemed "unclear."

4. In addition to affirmative action, another salient example is the debate over social welfare that has occurred since the 1980s. The argument for social welfare programs and public aid for people in poverty have had a marked egalitarian cast (see, e.g., Holyfield 2002). By contrast, the arguments against social welfare programs have had a significant libertarian flavor (see, e.g., Murray 1984). In education policy specifically, we can see this key conflict in policies such as school choice, bilingual education, and No Child Left Behind, to name a few (see, e.g., Petrovic 2005; Viteritti 1999; Wolfe 2003). Scholars write about neoliberal perspectives on education policy and reform (e.g., Hursh 2007; McGuinn 2006); I view those neoliberal perspectives as largely coming out of libertarian political theory.

5. As Mills (2005) and others have pointed out, Rawls's concern for equality of opportunity neglected to consider race. Despite Rawls' failing here, his work still applies to issues of race and opportunities.

6. Nozick is widely cited as such, despite the complexity of his ideas in *Philosophical Explanations* (1981), for example.

7. This idea was controversial not only because it exemplified a policy that shifted responsibility for welfare assistance from the state to private agencies but also because the proposal included federal funds given to the charities for that purpose. This brings up a contradiction for libertarian theorists, who would not agree with using federal funds for that purpose. My point with this example, however, is that it follows libertarian thought that the state is not responsible for providing such services.

8. Regarding this discussion of equality of opportunity and affirmative action, there is much overlap between the views of prominent libertarian and conservative thinkers.

9. See Gutmann and Thompson (1996, 19–21) for a particularly helpful discussion of the role of self-interest in motivating political action.

10. See Fryer and Loury (2005) for a discussion of the benefits of economic reasoning related to affirmative action.

11. Herein I use Young's (1990) definition of social justice as "the elimination of institutionalized domination and oppression" (15). Social policies and societal institutions directly influence the presence of social justice (Arthur and Shaw 1991).

12. The concept of "reasonable" herein excludes oppressive and hateful views. My understanding of "reasonable" follows from John Rawls's (2001) idea of the reasonable as a basic part of "society as a fair system of social cooperation" in which there is give and take and fair cooperation among equals (6).

CHAPTER FOUR

1. A promising experiment in Oregon aims to provide much more citizen input into the ballot initiative education process. In response to the types of criticism I raise here against direct democratic state ballot initiative processes, Oregon's Citizens' Initiative Review program started in 2011 after the governor created the Citizens' Initiative

Review Commission. The commission gathers together random panels of citizens to review and engage in dialogue about the ballot initiatives. Based on their dialogues, the panel members wrote up a Citizens' Statement that was published in the Oregon voters' guides sent to every household. Research on the Citizens' Initiative Review found that voters found those statements helpful and voter knowledge increased (Knobloch et al. 2014). This provides more empirical evidence for the deep democratic value of citizen dialogue.

CHAPTER FIVE

1. The example of a moral tragedy that I put forward was that of Proposition 209 in California, which effectively abolished affirmative action in the state. As a result, the educational opportunities for large numbers of minority students were severely diminished—the percentages of Latino and African American students enrolled at the University of California at Berkeley dropped immediately after the passage of Proposition 209.

CHAPTER SIX

1. Again I want to thank one of the manuscript reviewers for pushing me to think in this way and state it explicitly.
2. The discussion in this paragraph borrows from Gutmann and Thompson's (2004) analysis of the abortion debate.
3. See, e.g., Antonio et al. 2004; Backes 2012; Bowen and Bok 1998; Garces 2013a, 2013b; Hinrichs 2012; Sander and Taylor 2012.
4. See Hess and McAvoy (2014) for an excellent treatment of just how to do this.

REFERENCES

Adarand Constructors Inc. v. Peña, 115 S. Ct. 2097 (1995).

Andersen, Vibeke Normann, and Kasper M. Hansen. "How Deliberation Makes Better Citizens: The Danish Deliberative Poll on the Euro." *European Journal of Political Research* 46 (2007): 531–56.

Anderson, Elizabeth S. "The Democratic University: The Role of Justice in the Production of Knowledge." *Social Philosophy and Policy* 12 (2) (1995): 186–219.

———. *The Imperative of Integration*. Princeton, NJ: Princeton University Press, 2010.

———. "Integration, Affirmative Action, and Strict Scrutiny." *New York University Law Review* 77 (2002): 1195–1271.

Antonio, Anthony L., Mitchell J. Chang, Kenji Hakuta, D. A. Kenny, S. Levin, and Jeffrey F. Milem. "Effects of Racial Diversity on Complex Thinking in College Students." *Psychological Science* 15 (8) (2004): 507–10.

Appiah, K. Anthony. *Cosmopolitanism: Ethics in a World of Strangers*. New York: W. W. Norton, 2006.

Arthur, John, and William H. Shaw, eds. *Justice and Economic Distribution*. 2nd ed. Englewood Cliffs, NJ: Prentice-Hall, 1991.

Ash, Katie. "Education in Spotlight on Statewide Ballots." *Education Week*, October 8, 2008, 14–15.

Backes, Ben. "Do Affirmative Action Bans Lower Minority College Enrollment and Attainment? Evidence from Statewide Bans." *Journal of Human Resources* 47 (2) (2012): 435–56.

Baker, Julie. "Proposal 2: A Year Later." *State News*, November 15, 2007. http://www.statenews.com/index.php/article/2007/11/proposal_2_one_year_later.

Barabas, Jason. "How Deliberation Affects Policy Opinions." *American Political Science Review* 98 (4) (2004): 687–701.

Barry, Brian. *Culture and Equality: An Egalitarian Critique of Multiculturalism*. Cambridge, MA: Harvard University Press, 2002.

Belfield, Clive, and Henry M. Levin. "Vouchers and Public Policy: When Ideology Trumps Evidence." *American Journal of Education* 111 (4) (2005): 548–67.

Bell, Derrick. "Diversity's Distractions." *Columbia Law Review* 103 (2003): 1622–33.

———. *Silent Covenants:* Brown v. Board of Education *and the Unfulfilled Hopes for Racial Reform*. Oxford: Oxford University Press, 2004.

Bello, Marisol. "Affirmative Action May Be on Ballots." *USA Today*, December 27, 2007. http://www.usatoday.com/news/politics/2007-12-27-affirmative-action_N.htm.

Benhabib, Seyla. "Toward a Deliberative Model of Democratic Legitimacy." In *Democracy and Difference: Contesting the Boundaries of the Political*, edited by Seyla Benhabib, 67–94. Princeton, NJ: Princeton University Press, 1996.

Benjamin, Martin. *Splitting the Difference: Compromise and Integrity in Ethics and Politics*. Lawrence: University Press of Kansas, 1990.

Berlin, Isaiah. "The Pursuit of the Ideal." In *Moral Disagreements: Classic and Contemporary Readings*, edited by Christopher W. Gowans, 193–203. London: Routledge, 2000.

Bertrand, Marianne, and Sendhil Mullainathan. "Are Emily and Greg More Employable than Lakisha and Jamal? A Field Experiment on Labor Market Discrimination." *American Economic Review* 94 (2004): 991–1013.

Bonilla-Silva, Eduardo. *Racism without Racists: Color-Blind Racism and the Persistence of Racial Inequality in America*. Lanham, MD: Rowman and Littlefield, 2009.

Bowen, William, and Derek Bok. *The Shape of the River: Long-Term Consequences of Considering Race in College and University Admissions*. Princeton, NJ: Princeton University Press, 1998.

Bowler, Shaun, and Todd Donovan. *Demanding Choices: Opinion, Voting, and Direct Democracy*. Ann Arbor: University of Michigan Press, 2000.

Broder, David S. *Democracy Derailed: Initiative Campaigns and the Power of Money*. New York: Harcourt, 2000.

Brooks, Roy L. *Racial Justice in the Age of Obama*. Princeton, NJ: Princeton University Press, 2009.

Brown v. Board of Education of Topeka, 347 U.S. 483 (1954).

Burkhalter, Stephanie, John Gastil, and Todd Kelshaw. "The Self-Reinforcing Model of Public Deliberation." *Communication Theory* 12 (4) (2002): 398–422.

Bush, George W. "President Bush Discusses Michigan Affirmative Action Case." White House Press Release, January 15, 2003. http://georgewbush-whitehouse.archives.gov/news/releases/2003/01/20030115-7.html.

Button, Mark, and Kevin Mattson. "Deliberative Democracy in Practice: Challenges and Prospects for Civic Deliberation." *Polity* 31 (4) (1999): 609–37.

Button, Mark, and David M. Ryfe. "What Can We Learn from the Practice of Deliberative Democracy?" In *The Deliberative Democracy Handbook: Strategies for Effective Civic Engagement in the 21st Century*, edited by John Gastil and Peter Levine, 20–34. San Francisco: Jossey-Bass and John Wiley and Sons, 2005.

CBS. "Affirmative Action Lawsuits Hit Harvard and UNC." November 17, 2014. http://www.cbsnews.com/news/affirmative-action-lawsuits-hit-harvard-and-unc/.

Center for Equal Opportunity. Center for Equal Opportunity home page. Accessed August 30, 2013. http://www.ceousa.org/.

Chaffee, Steven H., and Stacey Frank. "How Americans Get Political Information: Print Versus Broadcast News." *Annals of the American Academy of Political and Social Science* 546 (1996): 48–58.

Chang, Mitchell J. "Does Racial Diversity Matter? The Educational Impact of a Racially Diverse Undergraduate Population." *Journal of College Student Development* 40 (4) (1999): 377–95.

———. "The Positive Educational Effects of Racial Diversity on Campus." In *Diversity Challenged: Evidence on the Impact of Affirmative Action*, edited by Gary Orfield, 175–86. Cambridge, MA: Civil Rights Project, Harvard University, and Harvard Education Publishing Group, 2001.

Chang, Mitchell J., Daria Witt, James Jones, and Kenji Hakuta, eds. *Compelling Interest:*

Examining the Evidence on Racial Dynamics in Colleges and Universities. Stanford, CA: Stanford University Press, 2003.

Chapa, Jorge, and Catherine L. Horn. "Is Anything Race Neutral? Comparing 'Race-Neutral' Admissions Policies at the University of Texas and the University of California." In *Charting the Future of College Affirmative Action: Legal Victories, Continuing Attacks, and New Research,* edited by Gary Orfield, Patricia Marin, Stella M. Flores, and Liliana M. Garces, 157–71. Los Angeles: Civil Rights Project at UCLA, 2007.

Chambers, Simone. "Deliberative Democratic Theory." *Annual Review of Political Science* 6 (2003): 307–26.

Clinton, William J. "Second Inaugural Address." In *Inaugural Addresses of the Presidents of the United States: From George Washington to George W. Bush.* Washington, DC: US Government Printing Office, 2001. http://www.bartleby.com/124/pres65.html.

Cohen, Joshua. "Deliberation and Democratic Legitimacy." In *Deliberative Democracy: Essays on Reason and Politics,* edited by James Bohman and William Rehg, 67–91. Cambridge, MA: MIT Press, 1997.

Connerly, Ward. "Achieving Equal Treatment through the Ballot Box." *Harvard Journal of Law and Public Policy* 32 (2009): 105–12.

———. *Creating Equal: My Fight against Race Preferences.* San Francisco: Encounter, 2000.

Contreras, Frances E. "The Reconstruction of Merit Post–Proposition 209." *Educational Policy* 19 (2) (2005): 371–95.

Cooper, Helene. "Obama Criticizes Arrest of Harvard Professor." *New York Times,* July 22, 2009. http://www.nytimes.com/2009/07/23/us/politics/23gates.html.

Corry, Jessica Peck. "Yes on 46 for Equal Opportunity." *Denver Post,* October 15, 2008.

Davidson, Kristen L., and Michele S. Moses. "Speaking across Difference in Community Dialogues on Affirmative Action Policy." *Equity and Excellence in Education* 45 (1) (2012): 217–36.

Deardorff, Michelle D., and Augustus Jones. "Implementing Affirmative Action in Higher Education: University Responses to *Gratz* and *Grutter.*" *Social Science Journal* 44 (2007): 525–34.

Delli Carpini, Michael X., Fay Lomax Cook, and Lawrence R. Jacobs. "Public Deliberations, Discursive Participation, and Citizen Engagement: A Review of the Empirical Literature." *Annual Review of Political Science* 7 (2004): 315–44.

Dennett, Daniel C. *Elbow Room: The Varieties of Free Will Worth Wanting.* Cambridge, MA: Bradford Books, MIT Press, 1984.

Denverpost.com. "Amendment 46—Discrimination by Gov Results." *Denver Post,* November 7, 2008. http://data.denverpost.com/election/results/amendment/2008/46-discrimination-by-gov/.

Dewey, John. *The Public and Its Problems.* New York: Capricorn, 1927.

Dickson, Lisa M. "Does Ending Affirmative Action in College Admissions Lower the Percent of Minority Students Applying to College?" *Economics of Education Review* 25 (2004): 109–19.

Donovan, Todd, Shaun Bowler, and David S. McCuan. "Political Consultants and the Initiative Industrial Complex." In *Dangerous Democrac7y? The Battle over Ballot Initiatives in America,* edited by Larry J. Sabato, Howard R. Ernst, and Bruce A. Larson, 101–34. Lanham, MD: Rowman and Littlefield, 2001.

Druckman, James N. "Media Matter: How Newspapers and Television News Cover Campaigns and Influence Voters." *Political Communication* 22 (1995): 463–81.

Dworkin, Ronald. *Sovereign Virtue: The Theory and Practice of Equality.* Cambridge, MA: Harvard University Press, 2000.

———. *Taking Rights Seriously*. Cambridge, MA: Harvard University Press, 1977.

Dyson, Michael E. "The Public Obligations of Intellectuals." *Chronicle of Higher Education*, December 5, 2003, B11–B12.

Edelman, Murray. *Constructing the Political Spectacle*. Chicago: University of Chicago Press, 1988.

Einsiedel, Edna F., and Deborah L. Eastlick. "Consensus Conferences as Deliberative Democracy: A Communications Perspective." *Science Communications* 21 (4) (2000): 323–43.

Elgass, Jane R. "University Lawsuit Gets Court Hearing." *University Record*, November 20, 2000. http://www.ur.umich.edu/0001/Nov20_00/3.htm.

Ellis, Richard J. *Democratic Delusions: The Initiative Process in America*. Lawrence: University Press of Kansas, 2002.

Ellsworth, Elizabeth. "Why Doesn't This Feel Empowering? Working through the Repressive Myths of Critical Pedagogy." *Harvard Educational Review* 59 (3) (1989): 297–325.

Epstein, David F. *The Political Theory of* The Federalist. Chicago: University of Chicago Press, 1984.

Erb, Robin. "Colleges Find New Ways to Retain Diversity." *Detroit Free Press*, December 10, 2007. http://www.freep.com/apps/pbcs.dll/article?AID=/20071210/NEWS05/712100377.

Farley, Amy N. "Democracy in Dispute? Ballot Initiatives, Education Policy, and Equal Educational Opportunity." PhD diss., University of Colorado Boulder, 2014.

Farley, Amy N., Matthew N. Gaertner, and Michele S. Moses. "Democracy under Fire: Voter Confusion and Influences in Colorado's Anti-Affirmative Action Initiative." *Harvard Educational Review* 83 (3) (2013): 432–62.

Feagin, Joseph R. *The Continuing Significance of Racism: U.S. Colleges and Universities*. Washington, DC: American Council on Education, 2002.

Feinberg, Walter. *On Higher Ground: Education and the Case for Affirmative Action*. New York: Teachers College Press, 1998.

Fisher, Robert J. "Social Desirability Bias and the Validity of Indirect Questioning." *Journal of Consumer Research* 20 (2) (1993): 303–15.

Fisher v. University of Texas at Austin, 133 S. Ct. 2411 (2013).

Fishkin, James S., and Robert C. Luskin. "Experimenting with a Democratic Ideal: Deliberative Polling and Public Opinion." *Acta Politica* 40 (2005): 284–98.

Fishkin, James S., and Steven A. Rosell. "ChoiceDialogues and Deliberative Polls: Two Approaches to Deliberative Democracy." *National Civic Review* (2004): 55–63. http://www.viewpointlearning.com/wp-content/uploads/2011/04/deliberative_democracy_w04.pdf.

Fiss, Owen M. "Affirmative Action as a Strategy of Justice." Faculty Scholarship Series. Paper 1322 (1997). http://digitalcommons.law.yale.edu/fss_papers/1322/.

Frank, Robert. "A Theory of Moral Sentiments." In *Beyond Self-Interest*, edited by Jane Mansbridge, 71–96. Chicago: University of Chicago Press, 1990.

Fryer, Roland G., Jr., and Glenn Loury. "Affirmative Action and Its Mythology." *Journal of Economic Perspectives* 19 (3) (2005): 147–62.

Fullinwider, Robert K. "Diversity and Affirmative Action." *Philosophy & Public Policy Quarterly* 17 (1 & 2) (1997): 26–31. http://journals.gmu.edu/PPPQ/article/view/265.

Gamble, Barbara S. "Putting Civil Rights to a Popular Vote." *American Journal of Political Science* 41 (1997): 245–69.

Gándara, Patricia. *Over the Ivy Walls: The Educational Mobility of Low-Income Chicanos*. Albany: State University of New York Press, 1995.

Gandy, Sara. "Foes Weigh Next Move Against Anti-Affirmative Action Initiative." *9News .com*, March 28, 2008. http://archive.9news.com/news/local/story.aspx?storyid=88903.

Garces, Liliana M. "Social Science Research and the Courts: Informing Post–*Grutter v. Bollinger* Developments in Higher Education Cases." *Educational Policy* 27 (4) (2013a): 591–614.

———. "Understanding the Impact of Affirmative Action Bans in Different Graduate Fields of Study." *American Educational Research Journal* 50 (2) (2013b): 251–84.

Garfield, Leslie Y. "The Cost of Good Intentions: Why the Supreme Court's Decision Upholding Affirmative Action Programs Is Detrimental to the Cause." *Pace Law Review* 27 (2006): 15. http://digitalcommons.pace.edu/lawfaculty/38/.

Gastil, John. *Political Communication and Deliberation.* Thousand Oaks, CA: Sage, 2008.

Gastil, John, and Peter Levine, eds. *The Deliberative Democracy Handbook: Strategies for Effective Civic Engagement in the 21st Century.* San Francisco: Jossey-Bass and John Wiley and Sons, 2005.

George, Robert P. "Law, Democracy, and Moral Disagreement." In *Deliberative Politics,* edited by Stephen Macedo, 184–97. New York: Oxford University Press, 1999.

Gerber, Elisabeth R. "Legislative Response to the Threat of Popular Initiatives." *American Journal of Political Science* 40 (1) (1996): 99–128.

———. *The Populist Paradox: Interest Group Influence and the Promise of Direct Legislation.* Princeton, NJ: Princeton University Press, 1999.

Goodin, Robert. *Reflective Democracy.* Oxford: Oxford University Press, 2003.

Gowans, Christopher W. *Innocence Lost: An Examination of Inescapable Wrongdoing.* New York: Oxford University Press, 1994.

———. *Moral Dilemmas.* New York: Oxford University Press, 1987.

Graber, Doris A., ed. *Media Power in Politics.* 3rd ed. Washington, DC: Congressional Quarterly Press, 1994.

Graham, Hugh Davis. *The Civil Rights Era: Origins and Development of National Policy, 1960–1972.* New York: Oxford University Press, 1990.

Gratz v. Bollinger, 539 U.S. 244 (2003).

Graves, Julie. "Talk amongst Ourselves: Examining How Heterosexual Adults Form and Transform Perspectives about Homosexuality through Dialogue with One Another." PhD diss., University of Colorado Boulder, 2013.

Green, Philip. *Equality and Democracy.* New York: New Press, 1998.

Grutter v. Bollinger, 539 U.S. 306 (2003).

Guetzloe, Douglas M. "Initiative Politics: A Useful Blend of Vested Interests and Citizen Politics." In *Dangerous Democracy? The Battle over Ballot Initiatives in America,* edited by Larry J. Sabato, Howard R. Ernst, and Bruce A. Larson, 30–32. Lanham, MD: Rowman and Littlefield, 2001.

Guinier, Lani. "Beyond Electocracy: Rethinking the Political Representative as Powerful Stranger." *Modern Law Review* 71 (1) (2008): 1–35.

———. *The Tyranny of the Majority: Fundamental Fairness in Representative Democracy.* New York: Free Press, 1994.

Gurin, Patricia. "Selections from the Compelling Need for Diversity in Higher Education: Expert Report of Patricia Gurin." *Equity & Excellence in Education* 32 (2) (1999): 36–62.

Gurin, Patricia, Eric L. Dey, Sylvia Hurtado, and Gerald Gurin. "Diversity and Higher Education: Theory and Impact on Educational Outcomes." *Harvard Educational Review* 72 (3) (2002): 330–66.

Gurin, Patricia, Biren A. Nagda, and Gretchen E. Lopez. "The Benefits of Diversity in Education for Democratic Citizenship." *Journal of Social Issues* 60 (1) (2004): 17–34.

Gutmann, Amy. *Democratic Education*. Princeton, NJ: Princeton University Press, 1987.

———. *Democratic Education*. 2nd ed. Princeton, NJ: Princeton University Press, 1999.

———. *Identity in Democracy*. Princeton, NJ: Princeton University Press, 2003.

Gutmann, Amy, and Dennis Thompson. *Democracy and Disagreement: Why Moral Conflict Cannot Be Avoided in Politics, and What Should Be Done about It*. Cambridge, MA: Belknap Press, 1996.

———. *Why Deliberative Democracy?* Princeton, NJ: Princeton University Press, 2004.

Hajnal, Zoltan, Elisabeth R. Gerber, and Hugh Louch. "Minorities and Direct Legislation: Evidence from California Ballot Proposition Elections." *Journal of Politics* 64 (1) (2002): 154–77.

Haycock, Katy, Mary Lynch, and Jennifer Engle. *Opportunity Adrift: Our Flagship Universities Are Straying from their Public Mission*. Washington, DC: Education Trust, 2010.

Hayek, Friedrich A., von. *The Constitution of Liberty*. Chicago: University of Chicago Press, 1960.

Healy, Patrick. "Berkeley Struggles to Stay Diverse in Post–Affirmative Action Era." *Chronicle of Higher Education*, May 29 1998, A31–A33.

Herzig, Maggie, and Laura Chasin. "Fostering Dialogue across Divides: A Nuts and Bolts Guide from the Public Conversations Project." Public Conversations Project, 2006. http://www.publicconversations.org/sites/default/files/PCP_Fostering%20Dialogue%20Across%20Divides.pdf.

Hess, Diana E., and Paula McAvoy. *The Political Classroom: Ethics and Evidence in Democratic Education*. New York: Routledge, 2014.

Hinrichs, Peter. *The Effects of Affirmative Action Bans on College Enrollment, Educational Attainment, and the Demographic Composition of Universities*. Washington, DC: Georgetown Public Policy Institute, 2009.

———. "The Effects of Affirmative Action Bans on College Enrollment, Educational Attainment, and the Demographic Composition of Universities." *Review of Economics and Statistics* 94 (3) (2012): 712–22.

Hobbes, Thomas. *Leviathan*. Edited by Edwin Curley. Indianapolis: Hackett, 1994.

Holt, Jim. "Export This?" *New York Times Magazine*, April 23, 2006.

Holyfield, Lori. *Moving Up and Out: Poverty, Education, and the Single Parent Family*. Philadelphia: Temple University Press, 2002.

Hopwood v. Texas, 78 F.3d 932 (5th Cir.), *cert. denied*, 518 U.S. 1033 (1996).

HoSang, Daniel M. *Racial Propositions: Ballot Initiatives and the Making of Postwar California*. Berkeley: University of California Press, 2010.

Hospers, John. "What Libertarianism Is." In *The Libertarian Alternative*, edited by Tibor Machan, 3–20. New York: Nelson-Hall, 1974.

Howe, Kenneth R. *Understanding Equal Educational Opportunity: Social Justice, Democracy, and Schooling*. New York: Teachers College Press, 1997.

Howell, Jessica S. "Assessing the Impact of Eliminating Affirmative Action." *Journal of Labor Economics* 28 (1) (2010): 113–66.

Hursh, David. "Assessing No Child Left Behind and the Rise of Neoliberal Education Policies." *American Educational Research Journal* 44 (3) (2007): 493–518.

Hurtado, Sylvia. "Research and Evaluation on Intergroup Dialogue." In *Intergroup Dialogue: Deliberative Democracy in School, College, Community, and Workplace*, edited by David Schoem and Sylvia Hurtado, 22–36. Ann Arbor: University of Michigan Press, 2001.

Jacobs, Lawrence R., Fay Lomax Cook, and Michael X. Delli Carpini. *Talking Together:*

Public Deliberation and Political Participation in America. Chicago: University of Chicago Press, 2009.

Jacobs, Lesley A. *Pursuing Equal Opportunities: The Theory and Practice of Egalitarian Justice*. Cambridge: Cambridge University Press, 2004.

Jaschik, Scott. "AP: More Pass and More Fail." *Inside Higher Ed*, February 11, 2010a. http://www.insidehighered.com/news/2010/02/11/ap.

———. "Strong Backing for Affirmative Action." *Inside Higher Ed*, April 1, 2010b. http://www.insidehighered.com/news/2010/04/01/affirm.

Kain, John F., and Daniel M. O'Brien. "*Hopwood* and the Top 10 Percent Law: How They Have Affected the College Enrollment Decisions of Texas High School Graduates." Paper presented at the National Bureau of Economic Research Meeting on Higher Education, Boston, MA, November 2001.

Kever, Jeannie. "White Sugarland Teen Sues UT over Admissions Policy." *Houston Chronicle*, April 8, 2008. http://www.chron.com/life/mom-houston/article/White-Sugar-Land-teen-sues-UT-over-admissions-rule-1678257.php.

Kidder, William C. "Misshaping the River: Proposition 209 and Lessons for the *Fisher* Case." *Journal of College and University Law* 39 (1) (2013): 53–125.

———. *The Salience of Racial Isolation: African Americans' and Latinos' Perceptions of Climate and Enrollment Choices with and without Proposition 209*. Los Angeles: Civil Rights Project/Proyecto Derechos Civiles, 2012.

Knobloch, Katherine R., John Gastil, Traci Feller, and Robert C. Richards Jr. "Empowering Citizen Deliberation in Direct Democratic Elections: A Field Study of the 2012 Oregon Citizens' Initiative Review." *Field Actions Science Reports* 11 (2014): 1–10.

Korrell, Harry J. F. "No Big Surprise: A Review of the Seattle Schools Case." *Engage* 8 (4) (2007): 11–17.

Kumar, Anita, and Rosalind S. Helderman. "McDonnell's Confederate History Month Proclamation Irks Civil Rights Leaders." *Washington Post*, April 7, 2010. http://www.washingtonpost.com/wp-dyn/content/article/2010/04/06/AR2010040604416.html.

Kymlicka, Will. *Contemporary Political Philosophy*. Oxford: Clarendon Press, 1992.

Lakoff, George. *Moral Politics: What Conservatives Know That Liberals Don't*. 2nd ed. Chicago: University of Chicago Press, 2002.

Lascher, Edward, Michael Hagen, and Steven Rochlin. "Gun Behind the Door? Ballot Initiatives, State Polices, and Public Opinion." *Journal of Politics* 58 (3) (1996): 760–75.

Leonhardt, David. "The New Affirmative Action." *New York Times Magazine*, September 30, 2007.

Long, Mark C. "Affirmative Action and Its Alternatives in Public Universities: What Do We Know?" *Public Administration Review* 67 (1) (2007): 311–25.

Long, Mark C., and Marta Tienda. "Winners and Losers: Changes in Texas University Admissions Post-*Hopwood*." *Educational Evaluation and Policy Analysis* 30 (3) (2008): 255–80.

Loury, Glenn C. *The Anatomy of Racial Inequality*. Cambridge, MA: Harvard University Press, 2002.

Lucas, Samuel R. *Tracking Inequality: Stratification, and Mobility in American High Schools*. New York: Teachers College Press, 1999.

Luo, Michael. "'Whitening' the Résumé." *New York Times*, December 5, 2009. http://www.nytimes.com/2009/12/06/weekinreview/06Luo.html?_r=0.

Madison, James. *Federalist*, no. 63 (March 1, 1788): 422–29. http://press-pubs.uchicago.edu/founders/documents/v1ch4s27.html.

———. "Speech in the Virginia Constitutional Convention," December 2, 1829. http:// www.constitution.org/jm/18291202_vaconcon.htm.

Magleby, David B. "Opinion Formation and Opinion Change in Ballot Proposition Campaigns." In *Manipulating Public Opinion: Essays on Public Opinion as a Dependent Variable*, edited by Michael Margolis and Gary A. Mauser, 95–115. Pacific Grove, CA: Brooks/Cole, 1989.

Mansbridge, Jane J. "The Rise and Fall of Self-Interest in the Explanation of Political Life." In *Beyond Self-Interest*, edited by Jane J. Mansbridge, 3–22. Chicago: University of Chicago Press, 1990.

Marin, Patricia. "The United States: The Changing Context of Access to Higher Education." In *Affirmative Action Matters: Creating Opportunities for Students around the World*, edited by Laura D. Jenkins and Michele S. Moses, 79–98. Routledge International Studies in Higher Education. New York: Routledge/Taylor and Francis, 2014.

Marin, Patricia, and Stella M. Flores. "*Bakke* and State Policy: Exercising Institutional Autonomy to Maintain a Diverse Student Body." In *Realizing* Bakke's *Legacy: Affirmative Action, Equal Opportunity, and Access to Higher Education*, edited by Patricia Marin and Catherine L. Horn, 219–39. Sterling, VA: Stylus, 2008.

Marin, Patricia, and Catherine L. Horn, eds. *Realizing* Bakke's *Legacy: Affirmative Action, Equal Opportunity, and Access to Higher Education*. Sterling, VA: Stylus, 2008.

Mason, Andrew. *Explaining Political Disagreement*. Cambridge: Cambridge University Press, 1993.

Matsusaka, John G. *For the Many or the Few: The Initiative, Public Policy, and American Democracy*. Chicago: University of Chicago Press, 2004.

McCloskey, Sharon. "UNC Sued for Use of Race in Admissions." *Progressive Pulse*, November 17, 2014. http://pulse.ncpolicywatch.org/2014/11/17/unc-sued-for-use-of-race-in-admissions/.

McDonnell, Lorraine. *Politics, Persuasion, and Educational Testing*. Cambridge, MA: Harvard University Press, 2004.

McGuinn, Patrick J. *No Child Left Behind and the Transformation of Federal Education Policy, 1965–2005*. Lawrence: University Press of Kansas, 2006.

McMillan, Jill J., and Katy J. Harriger. "College Students and Deliberation: A Benchmark Study." *Communication Education* 51 (3) (2002): 237–53.

Melville, Keith, Taylor L. Willingham, and John R. Dedrick. "National Issues Forums: A Network of Communities Promoting Public Deliberation." In *The Deliberative Democracy Handbook*, edited by John Gastil and Peter Levine, 37–58. San Francisco: Jossey-Bass, 2005.

Mendelberg, Tali, and John Oleske. "Race and Public Deliberation." *Political Communication* 17 (2000): 169–91.

Metzler, Christopher J. "Barack Obama's Faustian Bargain and the Fight for America's Racial Soul." *Journal of Black Studies* 40 (2010): 395–410.

Mezirow, Jack. *Learning as Transformation: Critical Perspectives on a Theory in Progress*. San Francisco: Jossey-Bass, 2000.

Mills, Charles W. "'Ideal Theory' as Ideology." *Hypatia* 20 (3) (2005): 165–84.

Milo, Ronald D. "Moral Deadlock." *Journal of the Royal Institute of Philosophy* 61 (1986): 453–71.

Moses, Michele S. "Affirmative Action and the Creation of More Favorable Contexts of Choice." *American Educational Research Journal* 38 (1) (2001): 3–36.

———. "By the People, for the People: Interrogating the Education-Policy-by-Ballot-

Initiative Phenomenon." In *Philosophy of Education 2009*, edited by Deborah Kerdeman, 177–86. Urbana, IL: Philosophy of Education Society, 2010.

———. "Contested Ideals: Understanding Moral Disagreements over Education Policy." *Journal of Social Philosophy* 35 (4) (2004): 471–82.

———. *Embracing Race: Why We Need Race-Conscious Education Policy*. New York: Teachers College Press, 2002.

———. "Moral and Instrumental Rationales for Affirmative Action in Five National Contexts." *Educational Researcher* 39 (3) (2010): 211–28.

———, ed. "Nonideal Theory and Philosophy of Education." *Educational Theory* 65 (2) (2015): 107–10.

———. "Race, Affirmative Action, and Equality of Educational Opportunity in a So-Called 'Post-Racial' America." *Kansas Journal of Law & Public Policy* 20, no. 3 (2011): 413–27.

Moses, Michele S., and Mitchell J. Chang. "Toward a Deeper Understanding of the Diversity Rationale." *Educational Researcher* 35 (1) (2006): 6–11.

Moses, Michele S., and Amy N. Farley. "Are Ballot Initiatives a Good Way to Make Education Policy? The Case of Affirmative Action." *Educational Studies* 47 (3) (2011): 260–79.

Moses, Michele S., Amy N. Farley, Matthew N. Gaertner, Christina Paguyo, Darrell D. Jackson, and Kenneth R. Howe. *Investigating the Defeat of Amendment 46 in Colorado: An Analysis of the Trends and Principal Factors Influencing Voter Behaviors*. New York: Public Interest Projects, 2010.

Moses, Michele S., and Patricia Marin. "Informing the Debate over Race-Conscious Policy." *Educational Researcher* 35 (1) (2006): 3–5.

Moses, Michele S., and Lauren P. Saenz. "Hijacking Education Policy Decisions: The Case of Affirmative Action." *Harvard Educational Review* 78 (2) (2008): 289–310.

———. "When the Majority Rules: Ballot Initiatives, Race-Conscious Education Policy, and the Public Good." In *Review of Research in Education* 36 (1) (2012), edited by Kathryn Borman, Arnold Danzig, and David R. Garcia, 113–38.

Moses, Michele S., Lauren P. Saenz, and Amy N. Farley. "The Central Role of Philosophy in a Study of Community Dialogues." *Studies in Philosophy and Education* 34 (2) (2015): 193–203.

Moses, Michele S., John T. Yun, and Patricia Marin. "Affirmative Action's Fate: Are 20 More Years Enough?" *Education Policy Analysis Archives* 17 (17) (2009). http://epaa.asu.edu/ojs/article/view/22.

Mouffe, Chantal. *The Democratic Paradox*. London: Verso, 2009.

Murray, Charles. *Losing Ground: American Social Policy, 1950–1980*. New York: Basic, 1984.

Nagda, Biren A. "Breaking Barriers, Crossing Boundaries, Building Bridges: Communication Processes in Intergroup Dialogues." *Journal of Social Issues* 62 (3) (2006): 533–76.

Nagda, Biren A., Patricia Gurin, and Shawnti M. Johnson. "Living, Doing and Thinking Diversity: How Does Pre-College Diversity Experience Affect First-Year Students' Engagement with College Diversity?" In *Improving the First Year of College: Research and Practice*, edited by Robert S. Feldman, 73–108. Mahwah, NJ: Erlbaum, 2005.

Nagel, Thomas. *Equality and Partiality*. Oxford: Oxford University Press, 1991.

National Issues Forum. "The Forum and the Framework." Accessed September 15, 2011. https://www.nifi.org/en/about.

Nederhof, Anton J. "Methods of Coping with Social Desirability Bias: A Review." *European Journal of Social Psychology* 15 (3) (1985): 263–80.

Nelson, Paul. *Narrative and Morality: A Theological Inquiry*. University Park: Penn State University Press, 2010.

New York Times Editorial Board. "Racial Equality Loses at the Court." Editorial, *New York Times*, April 22, 2014.

Noddings, Nel. *Caring: A Feminine Approach to Ethics and Moral Education*. Berkeley: University of California Press, 1984.

Nozick, Robert. *Anarchy, State, and Utopia*. New York: Basic, 1974.

———. *Philosophical Explanations*. Cambridge, MA: Belknap Press of Harvard University Press, 1981.

Nussbaum, Martha. *Cultivating Humanity: A Classical Defense of Reform in Liberal Education*. Cambridge, MA: Harvard University Press, 1997.

Oakes, Jeannie. *Keeping Track: How Schools Structure Inequality*. New Haven, CT: Yale University Press, 1986.

Oklahoma Secretary of State. "State Questions for General Election, November 6, 2012." http://www.ok.gov/elections/documents/Oklahoma%20State%20Questions%202012.pdf.

Orfield, Gary. Introduction to *Diversity Challenged: Evidence on the Impact of Affirmative Action*, edited by Gary Orfield, 1–30. Cambridge, MA: Harvard Educational, 2001.

Orfield, Gary, and Erica Frankenberg, eds. *The Resegregation of Suburban Schools: A Hidden Crisis in American Education*. Cambridge, MA: Harvard Education Press, 2012.

Orfield, G., Patricia Marin, and Catherine L. Horn. *Higher Education and the Color Line: College Access, Racial Equity, and Social Change*. Cambridge, MA: Harvard Educational, 2005.

Paguyo, Christina, and Michele S. Moses. "Debating Affirmative Action: Politics, Media, and Equal Opportunity in a 'Post-Racial' America." *Peabody Journal of Education* 85 (5) (2011): 553–79.

Parents Involved in Community Schools v. Seattle School District No. 1, 551 U.S. 701 (2007).

Pelletier, David, Vivica Kraak, Christine McCullum, Ulla Uusitalo, and Robert Rich. "The Shaping of Collective Values through Deliberative Democracy: An Empirical Study from New York's North Country." *Policy Sciences* 32 (1999): 103–31.

Petrovic, John E. "The Conservative Restoration and Neoliberal Defenses of Bilingual Education." *Language Policy* 4 (2005): 395–416.

Prah, Pamela. "A Look at State Ballot Measures for 2010." May 4, 2010. Project for Excellence in Journalism (with Rick Edmonds). *The State of the News Media 2004: An Annual Report on American Journalism*. 2004. http://stateofthemedia.org/2004/.

Public Conversations Project. "Constructive Conversations about Challenging Times: A Guide to Community Dialogue and Fostering Dialogue across Divides." Public Conversations Project, 2006. http://www.publicconversations.org/resource/constructive-conversations-about-challenging-times-guide-community-dialogue.

Ravitch, Diane. "Multiculturalism: E Pluribus Plures." In *Kaleidoscope: Readings in Education* (7th ed.), edited by Kevin Ryan and James M. Cooper, 458–64. Boston: Houghton Mifflin, 1995.

Rawls, John. *Justice as Fairness: A Restatement*, edited by Erin Kelly. Cambridge, MA: Belknap Press of Harvard University Press, 2001.

———. *Political Liberalism*. New York: Columbia University Press, 1993.

———. *A Theory of Justice*. Cambridge, MA: Harvard University Press, 1971.

Regents of the University of California v. Bakke, 438 U.S. 265 (1978).

Rich, Frank. "They Got Some 'Splainin' to Do." *New York Times*, July 18, 2009. http://www.nytimes.com/2009/07/19/opinion/19rich.html.

Rilke, Rainer Maria. *Letters to a Young Poet*. Translated by Stephen Mitchell. New York: Modern Library, 2001.

Roberts, Gene, and Hank Klibanoff. *The Race Beat: The Press, the Civil Rights Struggle, and the Awakening of a Nation*. New York: Knopf, 2006.

Rosen, Jeffrey. "The Dissenter." *New York Times Magazine*, September 23, 2007.

Rosenfeld, Michel. *Affirmative Action and Justice: A Philosophical and Constitutional Inquiry*. New Haven, CT: Yale University Press, 1991.

Ryfe, David M. "Does Deliberative Democracy Work?" *Annual Review of Political Science* 8 (2005): 49–71.

———. "The Practice of Deliberative Democracy: A Study of 16 Deliberative Organizations." *Political Communication* 19 (2002): 359–77.

Sabato, Larry J., Howard R. Ernst, and Bruce A. Larson. "A Call for Change: Making the Best of Initiative Politics." In *Dangerous Democracy? The Battle over Ballot Initiatives in America*, edited by Larry J. Sabato, Howard R. Ernst, and Bruce A. Larson, 179–90. Lanham, MD: Rowman and Littlefield, 2001.

Saenz, Lauren P. "Education Policy by Ballot Box: Examining the Impact of Anti-Affirmative Action Initiatives." PhD diss., University of Colorado–Boulder, 2010.

———. *The Status of Minorities and Women in Colorado's Higher Education System*. Denver: Piton Foundation, 2008.

Sandel, Michael J. *Public Philosophy: Essays on Morality and Politics*. Cambridge, MA: Harvard University Press, 2005.

Sander, Richard, and Stuart Taylor Jr. *Mismatch: How Affirmative Action Hurts Students It's Intended to Help, and Why Universities Won't Admit It*. New York: Basic, 2012.

Schevitz, Tanya. "Critics Say Plan Fails to Counter Image of Bias." *San Francisco Chronicle*, May 16, 2001, A4.

Schkade, David, Cass R. Sunstein, and Reid Hastie. "What Happened on Deliberation Day?" John M. Olin Law & Economics Working Paper No. 298, University of Chicago Law School, Chicago, 2006. http://www.law.uchicago.edu/files/files/298.pdf.

Schoem, David, Sylvia Hurtado, Todd Sevig, Mark Chesler, and Stephen H. Sumida. "Intergroup Dialogue: Democracy at Work in Theory and Practice." In *Intergroup Dialogue: Deliberative Democracy in School, College, Community, and Workplace*, edited by David Schoem and Sylvia Hurtado, 1–21. Ann Arbor: University of Michigan Press, 2001.

Schuck, Peter H. "Affirmative Action Is Poor Public Policy." *Chronicle of Higher Education*, May 2, 2003a, B10.

———. *Diversity in America: Keeping Government at a Safe Distance*. Cambridge, MA: Belknap Press of Harvard University Press, 2003b.*Schuette v. Coalition to Defend Affirmative Action*, 134 S. Ct. 1623 (2014).

Schultz, Marisa. "U-M Reports Slight Decline in Minority Enrollment." *Detroit News*, October 20, 2008.

Sears, David O., and Carolyn L. Funk. "Self-Interest in American's Political Opinions." In *Beyond Self-Interest*, edited by Jane J. Mansbridge, 147–70. Chicago: University of Chicago Press, 1990.

Shoemaker, Jason R. "Missing the Point: Befuddled by *Bakke*." *Wake Forest Law Review* 37 (2002): 1113–14.

Shook, John. "Dewey's Ethical Justification for Public Deliberation Democracy." *Education & Culture* 29 (1) (2013): 3–26.

Silver, Mitchell. "Irreconcilable Moral Disagreement." In *Defending Diversity: Contemporary Philosophical Perspectives on Pluralism and Multiculturalism*, edited by Lawrence Foster and Patricia Herzog, 39–58. Amherst: University of Massachusetts Press, 1994.

Simmons, A. John. "Ideal and Nonideal Theory." *Philosophy and Public Affairs* 38 (1) (2010): 5–36.

Smith, Daniel A., and Caroline Tolbert. *Educated by Initiative: The Effects of Direct Democracy on Citizens and Political Organizations in the American States.* Ann Arbor: University of Michigan Press, 2004.

Smith, Graham, and Corinne Wales. "Citizens' Juries and Deliberative Democracy." *Political Studies* 48 (2000): 51–65.

Smith, Mark A. "Ballot Initiatives and the Democratic Citizen." *Journal of Politics* 64 (3) (2002): 892–903.

Smith, Mary Lee, Patricia F. Jarvis, Walter Heinecke, Linda Miller-Kahn, and Audrey J. Noble. *Political Spectacle and the Fate of American Schools.* New York: Routledge, 2004.

Sobel, Lester A., ed. *Quotas and Affirmative Action.* New York: Facts on File, 1980.

Starr, Paul. *Freedom's Power: The True Force of Liberalism.* New York: Basic, 2007.

Steele, Shelby. *A Bound Man: Why We Are Excited about Obama and Why He Can't Win.* New York: Free Press, 2008.

Sterba, James P. *Justice: Alternative Political Perspectives.* 2nd ed. Belmont, CA: Wadsworth, 1992.

Stone, Deborah. *Policy Paradox: The Art of Political Decision Making.* New York: W. W. Norton, 2002.

Stratman, Thomas. "The Effectiveness of Money in Ballot Measure Campaigns." *Southern California Law Review* 78 (2005): 1041.

Sturgeon, Nicholas L. "Moral Disagreement and Moral Relativism." *Social Philosophy and Policy* 11 (1) (1994): 80–115.

Sunstein, Cass R. "Public Deliberation, Affirmative Action, and the Supreme Court." *California Law Review* 84 (4) (1996): 1179–99.

Tesler, Michael, and David O. Sears. *Obama's Race: The 2008 Election and the Dream of a Post-Racial America.* Chicago: University of Chicago Press, 2010.

Tessman, Lisa. *Feminist Ethics and Social and Political Philosophy: Theorizing the Non-Ideal.* Dordrecht, Netherlands: Springer, 2009.

Thernstrom, Stephen, and Abigail Thernstrom. *America in Black and White.* New York: Simon and Schuster, 1997.

Tolbert, Caroline, John Grummel, and Daniel Smith. "The Effects of Ballot Initiatives on Voter Turnout in the American States." *American Politics Research* 29 (6) (2001): 625–48.

Torres, Gerald. "*Grutter v. Bollinger/Gratz v. Bollinger*: View from a Limestone Ledge." *Columbia Law Review* 103 (2003): 1596–1609.

University of Texas at Austin. "Statement on Reinstatement of Affirmative Action in Admission." September 10, 2003a. http://www.utexas.edu/news/2003/09/10/nr_affirmative/.

———. "The University of Texas at Austin Proposes Inclusion of Race as a Factor in Admissions Process." November 24, 2003b. http://www.utexas.edu/news/2003/11/24/nr_admission/.

United States Census Bureau. "Boulder County, Colorado." *State and County Quick Facts,* 2010. http://quickfacts.census.gov/qfd/states/08/08013.html.

———. "Michigan." *State and County Quick Facts,* 2013. http://quickfacts.census.gov/qfd/states/26000.html.

Valentini, Laura. "Ideal vs. Non-Ideal Theory: A Conceptual Map." *Philosophy Compass* 7 (9) (2012): 654–64.

Vega, Tanzina. "Colorblind Notion Aside, Colleges Grapple with Racial Tensions." *New York Times,* February 24, 2014.

Viteritti, Joseph P. *Choosing Equality: School Choice, the Constitution, and Civil Society.* Washington, DC: Brookings Institution Press, 1999.

Vokey, Daniel. "'Anything You Can Do I Can Do Better': Dialectical Argument in Philosophy of Education." *Journal of Philosophy of Education* 43 (3) (2009): 339–55.

Wachbroit, Robert. "Public Deliberation and Scientific Expertise." *Philosophy and Public Policy* 18 (4) (1998): 17.

Waldron, Jeremy. *Law and Disagreement.* Oxford: Oxford University Press, 1999.

Walker, Margaret Urban. *Moral Understandings: A Feminist Study in Ethics.* New York: Routledge, 1997.

Walsh, Katherine C. *Talking about Race: Community Dialogues and the Politics of Difference.* Chicago: University of Chicago Press, 2007.

Weeks, Edward C. "The Practice of Deliberative Democracy: Results from Four Large-Scale Trials." *Public Administration Review* 60 (4) (2000): 360.

West, Cornell. *Race Matters.* Boston: Beacon Press, 1993.

Williams, Patricia J. *The Alchemy of Race and Rights.* Cambridge, MA: Harvard University Press, 1991.

Wise, Tim. *Colorblind: The Rise of Post-Racial Politics and the Retreat from Racial Equity.* San Francisco: City Lights, 2010.

Wolfe, Alan, ed. *School Choice: The Moral Debate.* Princeton, NJ: Princeton University Press, 2003.

Wong, David. "Relativism." In *A Companion to Ethics,* edited by Peter Singer, 442. Oxford: Basil Blackwell, 1991.

Wood, Peter. *Diversity: The Invention of a Concept.* San Francisco: Encounter, 2003.

Yankah, Ekow N. "The Truth about Trayvon." *New York Times,* July 15, 2013.

Yosso, Tara J., Laurence Parker, Daniel G. Solorzáno, and Marvin Lynn. "From Jim Crow to Affirmative Action and Back Again: A Critical Race Discussion of Racialized Rationales and Access to Higher Education." *Review of Research in Education* 28 (2004): 1–25.

Young, Iris Marion. "Communication and the Other: Beyond Deliberative Democracy." In *Democracy and Difference: Contesting the Boundaries of the Political,* edited by Seyla Benhabib, 120–35. Princeton, NJ: Princeton University Press, 1996.

———. *Inclusion and Democracy.* Oxford: Oxford University Press, 2000.

———. *Justice and the Politics of Difference.* Princeton, NJ: Princeton University Press, 1990.

Zetzer, Heidi A. "White Out." In *Explorations in Privilege, Oppression, and Diversity,* edited by Sharon K. Anderson and Valerie A. Middleton, 3–16. Independence, KY: Thomson/Cengage Learning, 2005.

Zúñiga, Ximena, Biren A. Nagda, Mark Chesler, and Adena Cytron-Walker. "Intergroup Dialogue in Higher Education: Meaningful Learning about Social Justice." *ASHE Higher Education Report* 32 (4) (2007).